COLLECTED WORKS OF CHARLES BERG

I0127735

Volume 7

FEAR, PUNISHMENT ANXIETY AND THE WOLFENDEN REPORT

FEAR, PUNISHMENT ANXIETY AND THE WOLFENDEN REPORT

CHARLES BERG

Routledge
Taylor & Francis Group

LONDON AND NEW YORK

First published in 1959 by George Allen & Unwin Ltd

This edition first published in 2022
by Routledge
4 Park Square, Milton Park, Abingdon, Oxon OX14 4RN

and by Routledge
605 Third Avenue, New York, NY 10158

Routledge is an imprint of the Taylor & Francis Group, an informa business

British Library Cataloguing in Publication Data
A catalogue record for this book is available from the British Library

ISBN: 978-1-032-16970-5 (Set)
ISBN: 978-1-003-25348-8 (Set) (ebk)
ISBN: 978-1-032-17242-2 (Volume 7) (hbk)
ISBN: 978-1-032-17246-0 (Volume 7) (pbk)
ISBN: 978-1-003-25246-7 (Volume 7) (ebk)

DOI: 10.4324/9781003252467

Publisher's Note
The publisher has gone to great lengths to ensure the quality of this reprint but points out that some imperfections in the original copies may be apparent.

Disclaimer
The publisher has made every effort to trace copyright holders and would welcome correspondence from those they have been unable to trace.

This book is a re-issue originally published in 1948. The language used is a reflection of its era and no offence is meant by the Publishers to any reader by this re-publication.

CHARLES BERG

Fear, Punishment Anxiety and the Wolfenden Report

Ruskin House

GEORGE ALLEN & UNWIN LTD

MUSEUM STREET LONDON

ACKNOWLEDGMENTS

The paper on 'The Psychology of Punishment' first appeared in *The British Journal of Medical Psychology* in 1945, and was subsequently reprinted in *The Yearbook of Psychoanalysis*, 1946. The paper on 'The Fundamental Nature of Anxiety' was based on a lecture given to the Psychiatric Discussion Circle at the Cassel Hospital, London, on February 3, 1950, and was published in *The British Journal of Medical Psychology* in 1951, while 'Fear—Normal and Abnormal' was published in *The Medical Press* of May 21, 1952. We are indebted to the Editors of all these Journals for their permission to include the papers in this book.

CONTENTS

I

The Wolfenden Report
on Homosexual Offences

IN GREAT BRITAIN, on the 4th August 1954, a Committee was appointed by the Government to submit a report on the law and practice relating to homosexual offences, and prostitution.

The Chairman was Sir John Wolfenden, Vice-Chancellor of Reading University, and the fifteen members included two judges of the High Court, three women, two Members of Parliament, two doctors, lawyers and ministers of religion. In the case of homosexuality the assignment was somewhat different, as the Committee were asked at the same time to consider the *treatment* of persons convicted of such offences by the courts.

This Committee presented its report in September 1957, after sixty-two meetings, more than half of which were devoted to the oral examination of 'witnesses'. It was careful to point out that its terms of reference were concerned throughout with the *law*, and offences against it, with what were the essential elements of a criminal offence, based upon the moral, social and cultural standards of society, law and public opinion, rather than on the psychological factors responsible for a particular form of behaviour. In other words, the emphasis was upon the overt or avowed (or pretended) psychology of the public (public opinion), as expressed in law, and not upon the psycho-pathology of the offender or the offence.

Nevertheless, in the course of their investigations, the Committee naturally found it unavoidable to examine certain aspects of the psychology of homosexuality, although these aspects of its investigation are not officially emphasised in its report. For instance, it declares that it found it important to make a clear distinction between 'homosexuality' and 'homosexual offences'. It says (page eleven of the Report): 'There is a further problem how widely the description "homosexual" should be applied. According to the psychoanalytical school, a homosexual component (sometimes conscious, often not) exists in everybody; and if this is correct homosexuality in this sense is universal. Without going so far as to accept this view *in toto*, it is possible to realise that the issue of latent homosexuality . . . is relevant to any assessment of the frequency of occurrence of the condition of homosexuality.'

Naturally it was not long before the Committee, consisting largely of lawyers, J.P's, M.P's and clergy, obviously found itself in difficulties. These difficulties remained or increased throughout its deliberations, and had something to do with the resignations of two of its members, and the reservations of about half the remainder. Their difficulties, with emphasis on their task of defining what was or was not a crime, legal meanings and legal sanctions and punishments, naturally led to the familiar juridicial preoccupation of hair-splitting, particularly in regard to the meanings of words—was homosexuality a 'disease' or was it not a 'disease'—and such irrelevant speculations, tending to ignore (but not altogether) what one would have thought to be the essential need to find out everything about it, including particularly its *meaning*, its psychopathology and its aetiology. (It is noteworthy that there was not one psychoanalyst on the Committee.) As they were of course unaware of the meaning, psychopathology and aetiology of *their own* attitudes, defensive mechanisms, and biases, it is inevitable that they should get into increasing difficulties. By the time we have examined their work, we may come to the conclusion that *all* of them should have resigned. However, within their limitations they are intelligent, well-educated people, and are honestly doing their best to integrate, explain and to make 'recommendations' (!) in connection with a phenomenon which they are, by nature of the unanalysed, civilisation-indoctrinated mind, incapable of understanding.

Most reviewers of the Wolfenden Report seem to have started at the end, rushing into a recital of the 'recommendations' before considering the process of arriving at these recommendations. The most revolutionary and 'controversial' of these 'recommendations' is that: 'homosexual behaviour between consenting adults in private be no longer a criminal offence' (the age of consent is specified as twenty-one years). It took a great deal of controversial discussion regarding the differentiations between 'private sin' and 'the business of the law' to pass this recommendation, and it may be noted that one member of the Committee, Mr. Adair, took great pains to dissociate himself from it, writing six closely-printed pages (pp. 117-123) to justify his disagreement. To the credit of the Committee, the majority of its members emphasised (para. 61): 'the importance which society and the law ought to give to individual freedom of choice and action in matters of private morality. Unless a deliberate attempt is to be made by society, acting through the agency of the law, to equate the sphere of crime with that of sin, there must remain a realm of private morality and immorality which is, in brief and crude terms, not the law's business. To say this is not to condone or encourage private immorality. On the contrary, to emphasise the personal and private nature of moral or immoral conduct is to emphasise the personal and private responsibility of the individual for his own actions, and that is a responsibility which a mature agent can property be expected to carry for himself without the threat of punishment from the law.'

Like many of the observations in this Report, we may say that the reasoning and breadth of view are commendable. I can only add that it is a pity the Committee do not extend the reasoning above quoted to the entire subject of the punishment for homosexual acts which are free from any element of *assault* (a separate crime), in which case a great step forward could have been made. For instance, to my mind the law should be concerned with safeguarding the liberty of the individual, quite irrespective of whether this liberty is infringed upon by threats, blackmail, robbery, unwanted interference, assault, decent or indecent, heterosexual or homosexual. If the law is going to act other than according to these principles, it itself is exercising an unwarranted interference with the liberty of the individual, and is therefore no doubt quite justly regarded by many of its victims as the criminal. I remember the case of a trembling, sweating, anxiety-ridden little man in the forties, who was brought to me by another homosexual on account of his incapacity, owing to his neurotic Anxiety State. The first story he told me was that ten years ago in a darkened car, well off the road and hidden amongst the trees of Epping Forest, he was 'spooning' with a man friend, a little older than himself. Suddenly all the doors were flung open and the interior of the car illuminated with powerful electric torches. Both men were arrested and finally, after they had been induced to incriminate many other persons, received five years' imprisonment each.

The point of this story is that so far as this man's psychology was concerned, he could no more see the wrong, leave alone the 'criminality', of 'spooning' with his man friend in what he considered to be privacy, than the average heterosexual man could see in 'spooning' with his girl friend or fiancée, or for that matter, wife. After all, this was his sexual pattern, and he had been living according to it in greater or lesser degrees for the whole of his life. However, he was not very strong-minded, and the action of the law had greatly shaken him, even to the extent of causing him to wonder whether his whole concept of morality was entirely 'off the rails'. In psychological language one must say that the firm and confident action of the law had so stimulated his superego that he had been overwhelmed with fear—of *it*, that is to say, with guilt feelings and anxiety. It had caused him to wonder, and later on to feel, that five years' imprisonment was not enough, and that he deserved the extreme penalty. Indeed, since his arrest he had been near to suicide on several occasions, the last one of which would have been successful had it not been for the timely intrusion of the kind homosexual friend who had brought him to consult me.

The recommendation that homosexual behaviour between consenting adults in private be no longer a criminal offence is broached as early as Section 62 in the Report, and is singled out as the first of the recommendations under Section 355. Admittedly none of the other recommendations is revolutionary, although I suppose jurists could be controversial over the most minor quibbles. Further recommendations (of comparatively minor interest) include (No. XIII) that the prosecution of any homosexual offence more than twelve months old be barred by statute. But this is watered down by the inclusion of 'except for indecent assaults'. Also [No. (iv) of the recommendations under Section 355], no proceedings should be taken in respect of any homosexual act (other than an indecent assault) committed in private by a person *under twenty-one*, except by the Director of Public Prosecutions or with the sanction of the

Attorney-General. (No. VI) The term 'brothel' should include premises used for homosexual practices.

The only remaining recommendation of the eighteen listed which seems to me to deserve any attention is number (vii), 'that there be introduced revised maximum penalties in respect of buggery, gross indecency and indecent assaults'. These are discussed under paragraphs 90 and 91, and consist in general of an increase of the existing, already fantastic severity of the punishments. For instance [para. 91 (c)]: 'Gross indecency committed by a man over twenty-one with a person of or above the age of sixteen but below the age of twenty-one, in circumstances not amounting to an indecent assault . . . ', the suggested maximum penalty for this is increased to five years' imprisonment. According to para. 92, this is designed to protect the young (i.e. between sixteen and twenty-one) because of 'the danger of emotional or psychological damage'.

However, before coming to a discussion of the 'final recommendations', let us go through the Report more systematically, though I shall have to be extremely brief to avoid tediousness and boredom, as so much that the Committee have to say consists in little more than platitudes. They ask (para. 13) 'what are the essential elements of a criminal offence?' and admit an inability to answer the question. Nevertheless, this does not prevent them from muddling through on their 'own formulation'. This includes 'to provide sufficient safeguards against exploitation and corruption of others, particularly those who are specially vulnerable'. One cannot disagree, but is tempted to reflect that such persons are always taken advantage of in every walk of life, one way or another, hence the worthy task may prove impossible. The strong arm of father or mother is often the only safeguard.

Law, regarded as a means of leading and fortifying public opinion (para. 16), creates difficulties, as the Committee found it impossible to discover 'an unquivocal "public opinion", and we have felt bound to try to reach conclusions for ourselves'. In other words, according to one's own pro or anti emotionally determined biases.

The Committee have discovered (para. 22) that homosexuality is not an ' "all or none" condition. . . . All gradations can exist from apparently exclusive homosexuality . . . to apparently exclusive heterosexuality'. They add: 'though in the latter case there may be transient and minor homosexual inclinations, for instance in adolescence'. Nevertheless this Committee of fifteen (or thirteen) learned men and women is apparently too nervous or too weak or too stupid to demand any alteration in the existing criminal law, which it seems would send the unfortunate victim of one of these 'transient and minor homosexual inclinations' to a long term of imprisonment, or worse. To the analyst it is well known that some persons reach 'adolescence' comparatively late in life, and indeed some appear never to grow out of it. The Committee agrees 'that a transient homosexual phase in development is very common and should usually cause neither surprise nor concern'. But three years in Borstal probably will!

It was found on statistical investigation that a large group of homosexuals averaged fifteen criminal acts a year each. According to this, the ratio of undiscovered criminal acts to those discovered by the police would be in the order of 2,500 to 1. This rockets to the skies in the Kinsey findings that within the age-group twenty-one to thirty, the ratio is 30,000 to 1. In the light of this it would seem that legal sanctions are somewhat irrelevant to the whole issue. The issue would naturally be security from detection, and this makes the barbarous severity of the punishments imposed upon that unfortunate 1 in 30,000 who is detected, all the more preposterous. It reminds one of the law in Saudi-Arabia, that a thief, if discovered, must have his hand cut off, and yet everyone knows that almost every person in Saudi-Arabia is a thief. Perhaps what would be relevant here is a psychological investigation of the source of all this pretence or denial. The Wolfenden Committee do not bring out these matters.

It sounds almost as though the Wolfenden Committee said very sympathetically: 'Yes, we know, we know all about it. We know that everyone has homosexual potentialities within him or her (though we do not propose to admit it). We know also that something like thirty thousand illegal homosexual acts are committed to every one that is discovered. Nevertheless we propose to allow the law (long since divergent from modern enlightenment) to continue to inflict every penalty short of death for that one in thirty thousand acts which is discovered,

16

while the undiscovered remainder (29,999) go scot free usually because neither party felt he had anything to complain about . . . or realized that it was as much his doing as the other persons's.'

Whilst so non-committal in regard to ferocity of punishment and apparently not doubting its justification and validity, and even in some instances actually recommending an extension of the heaviest penalties, vd. paras. 91 and 92 (in spite of professed sympathy), it is interesting that the Committee is only too ready to accept unproven theories if they help to clarify its erroneous conceptions. For instance, they readily assimilate Dr Kinsey's formula of 'homosexual-heterosexual continuum on a 7-point scale, with a rating of 6 for sexual arousal and activity with other males only, 3 for arousals and acts equally with either sex, o for exclusive heterosexuality, and intermediate ratings accordingly. The recognition of the existence of this continuum is, in our opinion, important for two reasons. First, it leads to the conclusion that homosexuals cannot reasonably be regarded as quite separate from the rest of mankind. Secondly, as will be discussed later, it has some relevance in connection with claims made for the success of various forms of treatment.'

Perhaps what is so misleading about the Kinsey 7-point scale is that such a very large proportion of males belong, apart from pubertal and adolescent inclinations, to the o category (exclusive heterosexuality) and so large a proportion of the remaining four or five per cent belong exclusively to the No. 6 category (activity with other males only). The few drifters towards whom Kinsey draws such unmerited attention may nevertheless be useful in so far as they demonstrate the possibilities of flux and its relationship to development.

I think there is a much-needed tempering half-truth in this unproven theory, in spite of its being misleading. Some psychoanalysts will have absolutely nothing to do with it. On the other hand it does speak a truth about the *unconscious*, if a misleading part-'truth' about the actual sexual *behaviour* of persons upon which diagnosis is based. But here it should be remembered that some heterosexuals can behave homosexually—or pretend—and some homosexuals can behave heterosexually—without any change in their true sexual pattern.

If the Wolfenden Committee are so ready to accept even the

doubtful theories of Dr Kinsey (presumably because they make thinking easier), may I ask why they steer clear of some of his best-proven statistical theories? For example, after telling us that thirty-seven per cent of the male population has some homosexual experience in the course of their lives, and the surprising fact that 'seventeen per cent of the farm boys have animal intercourse', Kinsey (1948, p. 392), by the simple process of adding percentages (and mathematics is usually regarded as infallible), concludes: 'All of these, and still other types of sexual behaviour are illicit activities, each performance of which is punishable as a crime under the law.

'The persons involved in these activities, taken as a whole, constitute more than ninety-five per cent of the total male population . . . It is the total ninety-five per cent of the male population for which the judge, or board of public safety, or church, or civic group demands apprehension, arrest, and conviction, when they call for a clean-up of the sex offenders in a community. *It is, in fine, a proposal that five per cent of the population should support the other ninety-five per cent in penal institutions!*' (My italics.) I refer to this again in the later part of this book.

If the Wolfenden Committee had got as far as acceptance of this exposition of the late Dr Kinsey, they would of course have had no alternative but to pack up and go home, and have nothing more to do with this bogy-hunting nonsense, bogies which they cannot catch in any case . . . because they are bogies.

But perhaps we should give credit to these new arrivals into what to most of them must be a strange field of science, in that they manage to recognize a few well-worn truths, though it is more difficult to forgive their platitudinous expression of these. For instance, they recognize that (para. 24): 'there are some in whom a latent homosexuality provides the motivation for activities of the greatest value to society. Examples of this are to be found among teachers, clergy, nurses, and those who are interested in youth movements and the care of the aged'.

Nevertheless it would seem that this Committee would support a law which sentences one of these invaluable teachers, a teacher with a heaven-sent aptitude for the education of boys, an aptitude which no truly heterosexual man could exercise, to no less than life imprisonment for one slip from his sublimation to the instinctual source from which it springs.

Another truth which they appear to recognize, this time even in the face of considerable medical opposition, is that the fully established practising male homosexual will never be turned into a heterosexual person. One can say that he may be taught, or teach himself, to do the tricks, but very soon it will be revealed that they are only tricks without substance behind them, and he will find himself totally impotent—except with males. As the *British Medical Journal* (September 14, 1957, p. 631) reports, quoting Drs D. Curran and J. Whitby's contribution to the Wolfenden Report: 'the most likely and valuable effects of treatment will be helping the young man whose homosexuality is transient but who requires psychotherapy to help him past it. For the patient who is adjusted to being homosexual much less is possible; *no doctor could produce for the committee a "cured" case of complete homosexuality.'* (My italics.)

The Journal goes on to say that 'The committee stresses the need for planned research into all aspects of this problem, a view that every doctor will endorse.' Indeed, they do stress it (para. 216). They recommend in their chapter on preventive measures and research 'a research unit which would include, for example, psychiatrists, geneticists, endocrinologists, psychologists, criminologists and statisticians'. It does not mention who is going to pay all these highly skilled workers, and it does not mention that this is the sort of research that is going on in the course of all the trainings and treatments in every analytical consulting room, institution of psychotherapy, analysis, and in mental out-patient departments, etc., etc. Maybe the research is all the more scientific for being of a free-lance variety, and not subject to 'plannings' and institutionalisation.

Obviously the Committee are very far from having read or understood the enormous quantity of scientific literature on this subject. As regards every doctor endorsing a planned research idea, my rough guess is that if he had more knowledge of psychopathology, he might well suggest that the 'planned research' turns its attention to the other side of the picture, namely to the unwarranted and undue morbid anxiety that sexual deviation is liable to lead to degeneration and ruination. Maybe the only terrible thing it is liable to lead to is this penalty or five or ten years or life imprisonment. Perhaps if all that nonsense were removed, there would be less anxiety and less homosexuality. After all, this is a phenomenon like every other phenomenon, which nature has produced in the same way as she produces many other curious things.

However the Wolfenden Committee, in spite of their endless incongruities, are not entirely ignorant, perhaps thanks to their medical and other witnesses, of the fact that homosexuality is more of a bogy (which the heterosexual, and often the homosexual man is trying to exterminate), than anything else. They even go so far as to say that there seems to be no evidence that homosexuality causes the decay of civilization, or could cause Britain to degenerate or decay.

It seems likely that this has something to do with their first and only important recommendation (namely that 'homosexual behaviour between consenting adults in private be no longer a criminal offence'). They arrive at it through an extraordinary ramble of philosophical and legal thinking, in which a plausible attempt is made to distinguish 'sin', a religious concept, from infringement of the 'law', a secular matter. Apparently the public has little difficulty in the ordinary course of thinking and behaving in distinguishing between private and group freedom of thought and behaviour (we even go so far as to allow primitive tribes to retain their religious beliefs and customs), and the infringement of some of the liberty of some non-consenting person, whether in the form of assault or otherwise. But in this matter of homosexuality, it would seem that the horror of the concept or phantasy is so great that a tremendous fuse and endless arguments have to be adduced to suggest that the public should not themselves here be the aggressors and interferers, however satisfied all the other parties concerned may be not to be interfered with. Apparently society and the law do not feel the same compulsive need to interfere in any other form of behaviour, including heterosexuality—though there was a time when they did.

Preceding their famous recommendation, there is the following characteristic preamble of which I shall quote a small portion although I have mentioned it previously: 'Unless a deliberate attempt is to be made by society, acting through the agency of the law, *to equate the sphere of crime with that of sin, there must remain a realm of private morality and immorality which is, in brief and crude terms, not the law's business.'* (My italics.) And wiser still ' . . . to emphasise the personal and private nature of moral or immoral conduct is to emphasise the personal and private responsibility which a mature agent can properly be expected to carry for himself without the threat of punishment from the law'.

So far, so good, but I think we should not be distracted by one or two good points in the recommendations into forgetting the relatively enormous lost opportunities, and indeed the complete blindness to the opportunity of exposing the inadequacy of punishment (to put it mildly) as a treatment. Admittedly the public have to be protected from such persons who would interfere unnecessarily with the liberty of its members, but by the same token the homosexuals, like those who prefer cinemas on Sundays, should be protected from the unnecessary interference of the public.

In his recent book *Why I am not a Christian*,[1] Bertrand Russell says: 'Perhaps it is the essence of a wise social system to label a number of harmless actions "Sin", but tolerate those who perform them. In this way the pleasure of wickedness can be obtained without harm to anyone!' He goes on to say: 'The conception of Sin which is bound up with Christian ethics is one that does an extraordinary amount of harm, since it affords people an outlet for their sadism which they believe to be legitimate, and even noble.'

It is astonishing, in view of some of the material collected by the Wolfenden Committee, however superficial (for instance the Police Court cases, paras. 112, 129 et seq.) that the conclusions and recommendations should be so inadequate and in most cases so unsympathetic, or even savage.

I think this can only be explained on the basis of the phenomenon familiar to analysts, namely that while many of the deliberations have in them some feeling and sympathetic understanding, this is interspersed with, particularly when it comes to making a recommendation, a regression to emotionally determined thoughts and behaviour, belonging to the familiar level where everything is either good or bad, and there is no

[1] Allen & Unwin.

penalty too bad for the bad, indeed the gratification, if it can be 'justified' or rationalized, of the superego element in our unconscious conflict. A factor in this phenomenon is the familiar one of having conceded a little in favour of the id (probably felt to be the Devil), one has to put a proportionate emphasis on one's hostility to it, even to the degree of *increasing* some already absurdly retributive penalties.

In most social groups, and in a large proportion of commonplace social gatherings, anybody who talked in the tone of the Wolfenden Report would be promptly dubbed a prig or a fool, but it seems a general principle that when we parade ourselves in public, or appear in print, we must pretend to these exclusively superego principles. They are naturally accompanied by a clamping down on all the real sources of knowledge, both within us and without. Pretence and open eyes do not go together and no doubt the Wolfenden Committee missed a great deal, if not all, of very relevant material (for instance, not a single prostitute and few, if any, truly representative homosexuals, appeared to give evidence).

A leading venereologist, who tells me that he treats as many homosexual persons as heterosexual, and who has a very long experience, expressed two opinions which one would have thought sufficiently superficial to appear in the Wolfenden Report. His first was that an important factor in driving men to homosexuality was (a) fear of making a woman pregnant and (b) fear of venereal disease. (Later they learnt to their cost that venereal disease was at least as frequent amongst homosexuals as heterosexuals.) The other factor which he seemed quite sure was much more important than was generally appreciated was the economic factor. He said: 'A lot of these lads are not really homosexual at all. I should say perhaps eighty per cent of them. I don't mean just the homosexual prostitutes. They get into or maintain a homosexual relationship with a sugar-daddy just because it relieves them of their economic struggle. The genuine homosexual, of which there are relatively few, commonly shows a great lust which these others do not show.' (It should be mentioned that this subject of economics as a great 'danger' is touched upon in para. 97 of the Report.)

Certain points of similarity with normal heterosexual life appear to one in this connection, namely for instance that many women do not partake of sex because of genuine heterosexual desire but because it fits better into the economic system, and this naturally applies to marriage even more than to prostitution. A doctor probably sees more husbands complaining that their wives are frigid, than wives complaining their husbands are impotent (which usually means repressed homosexuality).

For instance, one would hardly expect anything scientific or reasonable to emerge from deliberations which are, from the word 'go', like many legal rulings in other fields, based on arbitrary premises determined by emotions, and therefore we get these absurd difficulties in practically every paragraph, if not in every line of the Report. For instance (para. 70), they admit 'to fix the age (of consent) at twenty-one (or indeed at any age above seventeen) raises particular difficulties in this connection, for it involves leaving liable to prosecution a young man of almost twenty-one for actions which in a few days' time he could perform without breaking the law', a ridiculous enough position. The Report remarks that the age of consent in heterosexual intercourse is sixteen, so it would seem that the male needs more protection than the female, and there are innumerable other little incongruities which result from these unscientific and arbitrary decisions, all tending to prove that between the interstices of reason, the repressed conflict works its way through to give vent to the sadism of the superego.

But the Report has the courage blatantly to say that though the maximum penalty for seduction of an immature female (i.e. under the age of sixteen) has no more than two years' imprisonment, the equivalent act with a boy under the age of sixteen is *imprisonment for life*. This is the maximum penalty as it stands at present, but the Wolfenden Committee recommend that it should not be altered. Its only revision of maximum penalties is in the direction of increasing them where possible. There is one apparent exception to this rule, but on examination it proves to be only apparent. It is that buggery be reclassified as a misdemeanour instead of a felony. This, as the Report points out, means only that classifying it as a felony would incriminate the doctor who is told about it, and of course homosexuals should be encouraged to confess and doctors to listen to them. In short, it is a reclassification designed to protect the doctor-patient relationship.

23

Lest some may feel that I have not substantiated my case of alleged incongruity both in deliberations and in recommendations in the Wolfenden Report, I will quote a sample of utterances that it is difficult to correlate rationally, though it is easy to see the unconscious mental mechanisms at work. As has been mentioned, resulting from the enlightenment gained from medical and other witnesses, the Committee concluded there was no evidence that homosexuality causes the decay of civilisation, or could cause Britain to degenerate or decay. It says (para. 98): 'It is a view widely held, and one which found favour among our police and legal witnesses, that seduction in youth is the decisive factor in the production of homosexuality as a condition, and we are aware that this view has done much to alarm parents and teachers. We have found no convincing evidence in support of this contention. Our medical witnesses unanimously hold that seduction has little effect in inducing a settled pattern of homosexual behaviour, and we have been given no grounds from other sources which contradict their judgment. Moreover, it has been suggested to us that the fact of being seduced often does less harm to the victim than the publicity which attends the criminal proceedings against the offender and the distress which undue alarm sometimes leads parents to show.

'We have, it is true, found that men charged with homosexual offences frequently plead that they were seduced in their youth, but we think that this plea is a rationalisation or an excuse, and that the offender was predisposed to homosexual behaviour before the "seduction" took place.'

Now listen to the *penalties* which the Committee recommend *and the reasons which it gives for them*: (1) Life imprisonment for a grave offence with a boy under sixteen (as now); (2) ten years for indecent assault (against the will of the partner, or with those under sixteen); (3) five years for a grave offence or gross indecency by an over-twenty-one with a youngster between sixteen and twenty-one; and (4) two years for a grave offence or gross indecency by a man under twenty-one with a consenting partner over sixteen, or in public.

These penalties are mostly increased to protect the young. With regard to their severity compared with penalties for equivalent behaviour against the opposite sex, the Report says:

'We are inclined to agree, but we feel that any step which might be interpreted as minimizing the seriousness of assaults on young persons is to be deprecated.' The incongruity of the recently formed opinion of the Committee, namely that homosexuality will not cause Britain to decay, together with the conclusions derived from medical evidence that seduction in youth is not the main cause of a person becoming homosexual, as against their almost lifelong emotional reactions as expressed in their other pronouncements, that any step which might be interpreted as minimizing the seriousness of assaults on young persons — obviously because this is what makes them homosexual and ruins them—brings out in a highlight the extraordinary muddle through which these unanalyzed persons had to work.

In other words they are saying on an intellectual or conscious level that they have found no evidence for the popular and police view that seduction in youth produces homosexuality, but in their unconscious they still *feel* (as they felt in adolescence that masturbation would lead to paralysis) that it does, therefore it *must* be exterminated, apparently by the most barbarous penalties, the equivalents of the sadism of the primitive superego. (Why don't people get themselves analyzed first, before tackling a problem which is so far beyond them?)

Many superficial aspects of homosexuality, of homosexual behaviour, of homosexual crime, and of crime related to homosexuality, are discussed in this Report. As in every field of human life and behaviour, it would seem that every form of expression of conflict has some place. There is a somewhat inadequate reference to blackmail, and the fact that private homosexual activities, being crimes, place the participants in the hands of those particular homosexuals, or pseudo-homosexuals, who are out to extort money from easy victims.

Listening to the natural homosexual, it would seem to some people amusing that he commonly does not associate his behaviour with anything wicked, sinful and certainly not criminal. Therefore it comes to him as a terrible shock when he finds that his partner is using the law for the diabolical purpose of extorting money under the most terrible threats imaginable. From some police cases on record it would seem on the other hand that the law, or the police, are inclined to regard the sexual activity as more horrible or reprehensible than the blackmail, and cases are on record where a man, complaining of this form of blackmail, found to his surprise that he was charged by the police with homosexual crime. Such a case is recorded under para. 112, case I, where after seven years' sexual relationship, one of the partners commenced to demand money. When the victim finally complained to the police, the Director of Public Prosecutions advised that both men should be charged with buggery. After pleading guilty they were each sentenced to nine months' imprisonment. Neither man had any previous convictions. Their activities had been entirely private.

It is recorded that of seventy-one cases of blackmail reported to the police in England and Wales in the years 1950 to 1953 inclusive, thirty-two were connected with homosexual activities, but of course everybody knows that a great deal of blackmail, particularly in this field, goes on which never comes to the notice of the police.

Importuning by male persons seems to be the only mis-demeanour liable to imprisonment for more than three months where the person charged cannot claim to be tried by a jury. Thus any man is subject to having his life ruined by police evidence alone, without trial by jury. The Committee recommends that this should be amended, para. 123 and page 115, number (xii).

Legal and police attitudes towards homosexuality are full of incongruities, many of which are pointed out in the Wolfenden Report. For instance, some local authorities make bye-laws regarding the conduct of persons entering or using their public lavatories. These bye-laws frequently provide penalties for indecent behaviour, and these apply to homosexual behaviour, in which case under the bye-law the penalty may not exceed a fine of £5. Of course if the accused is unfortunate enough to be prosecuted other than under the bye-law, there is no knowing what crushing penalty he may receive. It is recognized that these public lavatories are a happy-hunting-ground for many homosexuals, despite the obvious dangers involved. There is perhaps something in homosexuality more than in hetero-sexuality of an immature phantasy nature, which must be kept removed from any reality exposure or analysis in order to pre-serve its excitement and pleasure. It is, as it were, something thrilling—(sex) in the dark. In this connection it was put forward that there would be less public lavatory nuisance if the lavatories were better lit, but statistics showed that just as many offences occurred in very well-lit lavatories as in very dark ones. Homosexuals who loiter in lavatories can of course be any degree of nuisance according to the psychology of their victim, but I think it would always be found that if the 'victim' takes no notice of them whatsoever, they make no advance, beyond being there. It would appear that this is a particular form of perversion, not only in the active party, but also in the passive. One has even heard of people of great eminence who have flirted with this form of behaviour. One such gentleman, a bachelor, after a long and blameless life, just after he had retired, apparently instituted his own neurotic penalty (incidentally almost as sadistic as those instituted by the law). He got a severe left-sided torticollis (wry-neck), which nothing would put right. In consequence he had to walk with his head looking over his left shoulder, and practically feeling his way about. He would not have believed that sex had anything to do with it. Of course in a sense it had not, this was not sex, this was the opposite; punishment.

His history revealed that from an early age his only sexual pleasure had been that of standing in certain lavatories in the hope of feeling the man standing beside him, or being felt by him. He knew this was terribly dangerous, and for some reason he usually turned to the right when he entered a urinal, so that the entrance was on his left-hand side. During the moment of acute sexual excitement he would be watching over his left shoulder to see if anybody, in particular the lavatory attendant, was coming in. Thus the conflict between his pleasure phantasies and desires on the one hand, and his anxiety on the other, were joined. He was never caught, but when he reached the age of fifty-five, suddenly, it seems, guilt and anxiety won the day; he completely stopped all these debasing activities, went over to the other side of the conflict, was inclined to deny the whole story of his life, and to pretend that he had never felt any sexuality at all. But at the same time this extreme and painful torticollis descended upon him.

I telephoned the doctor who had sent him to me, and said: 'At fifty-five this may be a very long case, particularly as he is so full of resistances. Could you perhaps try some of your methods first? For instance, if you got him a masseur to massage his neck, and if some sublimated homosexual rapport developed between them, do you think that might be a quicker way of helping this poor man?'

The doctor, who was very *au fait* in these matters replied, laughing: 'Good heavens, doctor, I thought you would know better than that. Don't you know that it isn't the slightest bit of use unless it happens in a lavatory?'

Obviously there is a lot of psychology and psychopathology to be revealed in such cases, as there is in the case of men who prefer a succession of prostitutes, and of women, including prostitutes, who prefer a succession of unknown men. But if this psychopathology is unravelled, it may be found that it is merely divergent and is quite strongly interwoven with what is called normal sex or love and hate relationships.

From most of the cases that come to see a doctor or psychiatrist, it is clear that a great deal of conflict between their more or less compulsive desire, comparable to the heterosexual desire, on the one hand, and attempts to control or repress it on the other, have taken place. Of course this is obvious in such cases as the one just described, where it was finally revealed that his castrating superego won the life battle. Now this intra-psychic conflict goes through the mechanisms of most conflicts in the unconscious, that is to say it tends to be projected into the world of reality around it. Put rather too briefly one may say instead of eradicating the source of guilt feelings *inside us,* if we can find these 'wicked' tendencies in some *other* person, particularly if he has given himself away, we then have a scapegoat ready to hand. It is so much more comfortable to exterminate, put in prison for life, punish, and all that sort of thing, *somebody else,* than to suffer internally ourselves. At last we know where the sin lies, in that fellow, and we can let him have it, and thereby we escape, or we gratify at least one side or one part of our intra-psychic conflict. It is through such unconscious processes as these that there spring up such extraordinary phenomena as the witch trials and Inquisition. Sexuality has always been very near the witch or demon, and this is much easier to rationalize if it is homosexuality. But to maintain such attitudes as these without insight, and thereby of course to avoid the neurosis or prison ourselves, we have to create in our own minds this peculiar bias which prevents us from understanding. To my mind it can be regarded as a mass psychosis, as will be pointed out in great detail in a forthcoming publication of mine.

Finally, the Wolfenden Report gets on to what it is pleased to call 'the treatment of offenders'. We cannot blame exclusively the members of the Committee for the extraordinary muddle to which these deliberations lead, for the public in general, including the jurists and educated public, have never sorted out in their minds, or successfully examined, the scientific principles involved in crime and punishment, and in this instance what they presume to call 'treatment'. Even when the process is frankly called 'punishment', emotionally charged factors in the punisher are practically the only determinants that one can discover. There is some recognition of this in the Wolfenden deliberations, when they say, regarding the 'lack of uniformity in the treatment of offenders by the courts' (para. 177): 'While we are therefore not able to suggest any positive remedy, we call attention to the matter and to the desirability of the courts' dealing dispassionately with every homosexual offence, giving proper weight to the reformative as well as to the deterrent or preventive aspects.'

There is no doubt that the strongest emotional force involved though often disavowed (as in this instance) in punishment, is retribution or revenge. If somebody stamps on one's foot, one is apt not to deal 'dispassionately' with his offence, or to give proper weight to reformative, deterrent, or preventive aspects. One is more likely to kick him as hard as one can! And that is retribution. It is a natural emotional reaction and may have nothing reasonable behind it. Perhaps the Chinese were more frank about the phenomenon of 'punishment' or 'treatment'. Their ancient book of rites specifies only one main punishment —cutting off the head!

While various cultural developments commonly, but not always, preclude us from such overt and natural reactions, it may be that in our retention of life-imprisonment as a punishment (or 'treatment'), for instance for buggery with a boy under the age of sixteen, we are approximating as near as we dare to the natural, overwhelming emotion of retribution. Thus we see that the Wolfenden Committee, in considering 'the law and practice relating to homosexual offences and the treatment of persons convicted of such offences by the courts' [para 1 (a)], is working on a special branch of a subject, the general principles of which have not been clarified, and are thus already muddled up by unclear premises.

It may here be mentioned that it is obvious to the therapist, who has to wean people from neurosis, delinquency or psychosis, that the display of any form of hostility—and punishment certainly displays hostility—brings all therapeutic measures to an end. I am now more inclined to the opinion that fear, such as the fear of punishment, does or can have some deterrent effect—but not nearly so great as is popularly supposed. I once had a patient whom it was very difficult to cure of his mackintosh fetishism, but when he was arrested by the police for looking through the bushes in the rain at girls taking shelter in a women's park lavatory, was so terrified that he suppressed such impulses for at least six months. Fortunately the police could not begin to understand his motives, and so no charge was actually brought against him. Fear thus had a deterrent effect, albeit it produced an increase in his anxiety neurosis.

The question here may well be are we trying to win the abnormal person back to normality, or are we trying to protect society from the nuisance this abnormality causes? If merely the latter, then the Chinese were right, the surest way is to cut off his head . . . or send him to life imprisonment. If the former, we will almost certainly fail if we contaminate our treatment with anything such as punishment, which reveals hostility. The man already has an intra-psychic conflict and in getting us to punish him he is merely co-opting us into taking sides with one side of that conflict, maybe so that he can consequently enjoy greater freedom with the other side. The therapist's job may indeed be to save him from a too-dramatic dramatization of his conflict, such as suicide.

The difficulty that has to be faced by the community is the conflict between nuisance or injury to the public and the well-being of the individual, through which latter alone can therapeutic success be gained. No doubt most of us would say that the matter of first importance is to protect the public, hence we have the legal institutions of capital punishment and life imprisonment. But do not let us get confused between this public-protection motive, and therapy. The trouble is that not only do we get confused, but each motive is apt to exceed its assignment so that we get poking our noses in where the public have no business, and making our criminals, perhaps lest on the other hand we may be jeopardising the well-being of a large number of persons for the sake of one psychopath.

It is interesting to note that although the maximum punishments, particularly in regard to homosexual offences, seem to be so savagely out of proportion to the damaged caused, nevertheless in the courts themselves it is more usual (though not usual enough) to find 'justice', with the maximum punishment principle, tempered with mercy—if anything can be merciful after the public exposure of an individual's sexual practices. The Wolfenden Report tells us that though imprisonment is 'the punishment prescribed by law for homosexual offences . . . only a minority of homosexual offenders are sent to prison. For instance, in 1955 only thirty per cent . . . and in Scotland, during the same year, only thirty-seven per cent' (para. 149). It is noteworthy that this is not a very small percentage. Other 'treatments' and punishments included absolute discharge, conditional discharge, binding over, probation, and fine. It is noteworthy that 'thirty per cent of the persons convicted in 1955 of homosexual offences punishable with imprisonment were fined instead' (para. 158).

In the case of young offenders the equivalent punishments are Borstal training, detention in a detention centre, committal to an Approved School, committal to the care of a fit person, and attendance at an Attendance Centre. The last three are for offenders under seventeen years of age.

It seems to me possible that the discrepancy between the theoretically laid-down (maximum) penalties for homosexual behaviour and some of these relatively 'minor' executions is due to the fact that the court has had the opportunity of making the acquaintance of the accused, thereby discovering that he is not so terrible as the abstract conception paints him. One may add that were it possible for the punishers to mix freely in the lives of the alleged culprits, and really get to know them, their outlook, and even their way of life and delinquent behaviour, the compulsion to punish might increasingly give way to understanding and therapy, at least in a large number of cases. As

Barbara Wootton put it: 'The concept of illness expands continually at the expense of the concept of moral failure.'[1]

In passing it should be mentioned that the Wolfenden Committee rejected the proposition that homosexuality should be regarded as a 'disease'. They naïvely remark that 'to decide the most appropriate method of treatment of a particular offender is a much more difficult problem for the courts than the decision as to his guilt' (para. 169). I say 'naïvely' because I can think of no person or body of persons less well qualified to assess an 'appropriate method of treatment' than those associated with the courts. The whole atmosphere, like the chopping off of heads, is the antithesis of 'treatment'.

A similar statement is (para. 170): 'Apart altogether from any considerations of retribution the objectives of penal sanctions are deterrence, prevention and reformation'. The truth is that the act of punishment is determined by the reaction of retribution, which is powerful enough to brush all else aside. This 'criminal' act is then rationalized, and even sanctified, by the high ideals of 'deterrence', 'prevention' and 'reformation'.

It reminds me of a patient I once had, whose father (a jurist) used periodically to order him to come to his study (the next morning!) for punishment. He would be ordered to bend over the bed while the father delicately and lovingly removed his shorts and any underwear, and went on to stroke his behind before proceeding to the inevitable caning. To my mind there was little doubt that the father, like the son, was a repressed homosexual. But the point I wish to bring out here is that the father invariably sanctified his act by saying to the boy 'you must always remember that this is for your own good'. (Deterrence, prevention and reformation.) I can remember also the son's description of his reaction! It was only fear that kept him from murder. Is this the 'treatment' which the law institutes?

If we bear in mind the very small percentage of homosexual crimes which are detected by the law, one in thirty thousand, we may find it easy to believe that the deterrent which outweighs all others is the fear of detection. Perhaps it outweighs all others in the proportion of one to thirty thousand. In this case we may say that it really does not matter what these sanc-

[1] 'Sickness or Sin', *Twentieth Century*, May 1956.

tions and punishments amount to, execution or one's photograph in the local newspaper, they are all completely dwarfed by the danger of exposure and perhaps by the disgrace, etc., following such exposure. Thus the one concern of the delinquent, be it in the homosexual sphere or in any other, is that he shall not be discovered, particularly by the police. This brings one to the view that if discovery were always inevitable, be it in the sphere of homosexuality or in any other sphere of crime, then crime simply would not take place. Our conclusion may be that deliberation as to what you do with the mouse when you catch it is entirely irrelevant, because the first thing is to catch it. Are we just exercising a little game to express some of our unconscious tendencies and enhance our phantasy of omnipotence? Perhaps it would be better to have a Committee on how to apprehend crime or the criminal before we proceed to a discussion as to what to do with him. Otherwise he is, in nearly thirty thousand cases to one, prescribing and carrying out his own 'treatment'.

Another point the Wolfenden Committee brings out and debunks is the popular illusion that treatment is something which can take place in prison. I shall not go into details but they rightly come to the decision that it cannot. In any case, prison and treatment are incompatible.

No doubt there is something to be learnt from the Wolfenden Report, particularly if like most of the members we knew nothing to start with. For instance, it is brought out that the ordinary adult homosexual, who has integrated his sexual life with that of friendship, love or passion towards another adult male, is often just as shocked by the male who pursues lads of fifteen or under, as the average heterosexual man would be at a man who pursued young girls or children for sexual purposes. In short, to the 'normal' person, heterosexual or homosexual, paedicatio mulierum. The natural male homosexual resents very strongly any confusion of his proclivities or those of his friends with the abnormal 'perverted' proclivities of such a deviant. The latter are possibly more frequently apprehended and would therefore, in police courts and prisons, suggest a higher proportion of homosexuals than is truly representative. 'Of 1,022 men in prison for homosexual offences in 1954, no fewer than 590 (58%) were involved in offences against boys

C   33

aged fifteen or under.' It is noteworthy also that '236 of these had previous convictions for homosexual offences. Further, of the 1,022 prisoners, 211 (21·6%) had four or more previous convictions of one kind or another recorded against them and of these 102 (10%) had seven or more . . . the Cambridge survey indicates that two-thirds of the sexual recidivists under review had previous convictions for sexual offences only, and that generally there was a similarity between the repeated offences' (para. 202).

This last remark reminds the therapist that practically all patients who come to him for treatment, not only homosexuals but all those suffering from neurosis, and especially from minor psychosis, are incredibly resistant to giving up one iota of their beliefs, delusions, or reactive patterns. A patient once said to me: 'But doctor, if you take that murder impulse away from me, it will no longer be *me*. I shall have nothing to live for. I would feel already dead.' This may give us a slight conception of the resistance to even minor modifications, leave alone 'cure'. (Perhaps the Chinese were right!)

I do not know much about resistance to medical or surgical interference for therapeutic purposes, but as regards oestrogens (para. 209) a doctor who tried it on a transvestite patient whom I sent him, told me that the man refused to go on with the treatment *because it made him so miserable.* No doubt the surgical treatment of castration would tend similarly to make the victim miserable, though there are some countries where it is practised with the consent of the offender. The Wolfenden Committee rejected it on the grounds that the operation removes neither the desires nor the ability to fulfil them, for instance in the case of a passive male homosexual.

The two doctors on the Committee (Curran and Whitby) emphasise some interesting points. For instance, they rightly say that 'the same criminal act may be committed as a piece of adolescent experimentation; or it may be the result of temporary or permanent mental or physical disorder or disease; or it may be part of the individual's life style'. In short, 'that there is a great variety of problems, that the significance of offences varies with the individual offender . . . that individual cases may require individual treatment, does not always lead to their application in practice. . . . The large group of youngsters and

young men with what is often called "transitional" homosexuality is especially important' (pages 72, 73 et seq.).
They quote Dr T. C. N. Gibbens (in a paper entitled 'The
Sexual Behaviour of Young Criminals'), as saying, after studying two hundred Borstal lads: 'Perhaps the most important
point that has to be made about homosexuality is that it should
not be considered in isolation from heterosexuality. The issues
are those of sexuality, with homosexual and heterosexual components in each case.'

Drs Curran and Whitby emphasize also that many males
pass through a homosexual phase satisfactorily and without
medical help. It makes one reflect that it is rather unfortunate
if any of these are apprehended during this transient phase,
and thereby perhaps prevented from leading a normal sexual
life.

The doctors think a high proportion of homosexual cases
have associated psychiatric abnormality. They agree with the
recommendation that, with the patient's consent, oestrogen
treatment should be permitted in suitable cases in prison. They
recommend also a more extended resort to probation with a
condition of medical treatment, as mentioned in para. 200,
although evidence is that the treatment under these auspices is
unsuccessful.

Although the Committee generally agree that the duration of
a prison sentence should not be decided on purely therapeutic
grounds (page 76), it is added that 'our medical witnesses were
unanimous that cases did occur in which a prison sentence
could have therapeutic value'. I am perfectly certain that this
is a fond delusion. The only 'therapeutic value' there can
possibly be is that of the patient either being frightened and
thereby deterred in his overt freedom, or/and his deceiving the
doctors and perhaps even himself for the sake of 'peace of mind'.
After all, you *must* go over to the side of the people who can
apprehend and imprison you like this, even if it gives you a
state of internal tension or nervous breakdown.

There are perhaps a few other 'discoveries' which should be
tabulated. The Committee agrees that most homosexual
behaviour is due to the existence of the 'homosexual propensity'
in a greater or lesser degree in one or both of the participants.
However, they conclude that they have no idea what this homo-

sexual propensity is. If this is the basis of the whole trouble, perhaps they should have ceased work on that note.

'To ensure that men guilty of homosexual offences with boys or girls are not allowed to continue in the teaching profession' (para. 219) is of course only common sense, and no doubt relevant to the principle of prevention, provided a distinction is made between the ordinary 'mature' male homosexual, who consorts with adults, and the paederast. Another common sense preventive measure, or at least precautionary measure, is the bye-law prevalent in some places in Scotland, making it an offence to stay unduly long in a public lavatory (para. 220).

After over three years of deliberations, the members of the Wolfenden Committee arrived at the following recommendations, regarding the law and practice relating to homosexual offences, and the treatment of persons convicted of such offences by the courts. Although we have singled out the only important or revolutionary one of these, and lightly dismissed most of the others as trivial, it may be desired by those who have not had access to the Wolfenden Report to know exactly what these were. The Committee tabulated them as follows:

1. 'That homosexual behaviour between consenting adults in private be no longer a criminal offence" (para. 62).
2. 'That questions relating to "consent" and "in private" be decided by the same criteria as apply in the case of heterosexual acts between adults' (paras. 63, 64).
3. 'That the age of "adulthood" for the purposes of the proposed change in the law be fixed at twenty-one' (para. 71).
   (As mentioned there was a lot of discussion about this as the age of consent in heterosexual intercourse is sixteen, but finally twenty-one was decided upon.)
4. 'That no proceedings be taken in respect of any homosexual act (other than an indecent assault) committed in private by a person under twenty-one, except by the Director of Public Prosecutions or with the sanction of the Attorney-General' (para. 72).
5. 'That the law relating to living on the earnings of prostitution be applied to the earnings of male, as well as female, prostitution' (para. 76).
   (It is doubtful whether any person, female or male, is

36

really in the position of 'Slave-labour' imagined by some members of the public.)

6. 'That the law be amended, if necessary, so as to make it explicit that the term "brothel" includes premises used for homosexual practices' (para. 76).

7. 'That there be introduced revised maximum penalties in respect of buggery, gross indecency and indecent assaults' (paras. 90, 91).

8. 'That buggery be re-classified as a misdemeanour' (para. 94).

[As mentioned this was not to diminish the offence, on the contrary the penalties for buggery exceed those of any other form of homosexual act, starting with life imprisonment if with a boy under the age of sixteen, and five years' imprisonment for a boy above the age of sixteen, below the age of twenty-one (in circumstances not amounting to indecent assault — which carries ten years). This five-year imprisonment penalty is an increase recommended by the Committee on the present law. It would seem incongruous, as there is no penalty whatsoever for the equivalent heterosexual act with a consenting female of this age.]

9. 'That except for some grave reason, proceedings be not instituted in respect of homosexual offences incidentally revealed in the course of investigating allegations of blackmail' (para. 112).

10. 'That Section 29 (3) of the Larceny Act, 1916, be extended so as to apply to all homosexual offences' (para. 113).

11. 'That the offence of gross indecency between male persons be made triable summarily with the consent of the accused' (para. 114).

12. 'That male persons charged with importuning for immoral purposes be entitled to claim trial by jury' (para. 123).

13. 'That except for indecent assaults, the prosecution of any homosexual offence more than twelve months old be barred by statute' (para. 135).

14. 'That subject to any necessary special safeguards, managers and headmasters of approved schools be allowed the same measure of discretion in dealing with homosexual behaviour between inmates as that enjoyed by those responsible for the management of any other educational establishment' (para. 147).

15. 'That the organisation, establishment and conditions of service of the prison medical service be reviewed' (para. 180).
16. 'That a court by which a person under twenty-one is found guilty of a homosexual offence be required to obtain and consider a psychiatric report before passing sentence' (para. 187).
17. 'That prisoners desirous of having oestrogen treatment be permitted to do so if the prison medical officer considers that this would be beneficial' (para. 211).
18. 'That research be instituted into the aetiology of homosexuality and the effects of various forms of treatment' (para. 216).

The remaining thirteen members of the Committee, two, as mentioned, having resigned about eighteen months previously, signed these recommendations, six with reservations. As has been mentioned, Mr. Adair's reservation was a disagreement with the principal recommendation, number one, eloquently argued. The distinction between buggery and other homosexual offences was objected to by four members, including two ladies and the two doctors. Dr Whitby has some further reservations, chiefly aimed at making no distinction between buggery and indecent assault (carrying a maximum penalty of ten years' imprisonment), and in minor cases between buggery with consent and gross indecency (penalty two years' imprisonment). At the same time he stresses that the effects of homosexual seduction in youth have been greatly exaggerated. He says: 'whatever moral damage may be done, the effect of seduction over . . . the age of sixteen . . . is unlikely to be that of producing a homosexual deviation in one who is predominantly heterosexual' (page 125).

Dr Curran in his 'further reservation' carries these objections a good deal further. He would like to 'make the maximum sentence for indecent assault two years instead of ten years'. He emphasizes that ' "the law itself probably makes little difference to the amount of homosexual behaviour which actually occurs; whatever the law may be, there will always be strong social forces opposed to homosexual behaviour". These strong social forces are, I believe, specially operative in the case of paedophiliacs, whose conduct is universally reprobated, not least by other homosexuals. Paedophiliacs act in isolation from the homosexuals, and are not accepted in homosexual coteries or groups' (page 126).

In keeping with my views, Dr Curran goes on to say: 'I understand it has long been common ground in the opinion of those best qualified to judge that it is not the severity of the punishment that is most important for deterrence; it is the certainty—or high degree of probability—that punishment will actually result. If correct, this principle has special application to all homosexual crimes owing to the vast discrepancy between the number of criminal acts and the conviction rate. . . . Can it seriously be supposed that those who are guilty of indecent assault work out "betting odds" of this kind (the number of years in prison) before they indulge in their acts? And if they did, what deterrent effect would it be likely to have?'

And further: 'It seems to me that the sole, and very proper, justification for long sentences is to keep out of harm's way those who have repeatedly shown themselves to be public menaces and concerning whom nothing else, in the present state of knowledge, can be done.'

But it seems the length of the prison sentence is not motivated by such considerations, as Dr Curran points out in his following paragraphs, where he shows that thirty-two of fifty-four men sentenced to prison had no previous convictions, and no other offences were taken into consideration. He suggests that the severity of the punishments reveals principally retribution. I agree.

When Dr Curran suggests that in the present state of our knowledge nothing else can be done, I would like to add that what could be done is an alteration in our attitude. We protect the public from dangerous lunatics and mental defectives without bringing into the picture ideas of crime and punishment—or retribution. The attitude of mind is different, and much might be learnt from it.

Regarding importuning, Dr Curran says: 'I can see no logical reason why male importuning should be treated differently from female solicitation.' His further remarks are of interest: 'Males seldom importune other males who do not give them encouragement. Their activities are less obvious, and more subtle and discreet, than is the case with female solicitation. Consequently, as I believe, the general public greatly underestimate (as do the criminal statistics) the amount of male importuning that goes on. Further, the number of male importuners who are prostitutes is admittedly extremely small; very few male importuners are out for financial gain.' He does not consider that a relaxation of the penalties on male importuning would result in an increase or a public nuisance, as other members of the Committee appeared to think. He considers that the same safeguards and penalties as are proposed for common prostitutes would provide an adequate safeguard against the development of brazen activities on the part of male importuners which might be publicly offensive.

Doctors and psychiatrists, and of course particularly analysts learn so much of the private sexual life of their patients, that they cannot always maintain the horrified attitude of the layman and pretend that sexuality, even homosexuality, is something exceptional, perhaps something to be denied and certainly execrated. They have come nearer to recognizing that knowledge is the only answer to all the problems here presented. Nevertheless it would seem that even doctors and psychiatrists, presented with the atmosphere of the law-courts, and I think that the Wolfenden Committee presented much of such an atmosphere, are not immune, unconsciously at least, to the influence which this atmosphere has upon our ever-wobbling conflicts, even if they are on a conscious plane, that is to say a more superficial plane and reinforced by knowledge of that which the superego denies. This seems to me the only explanation as to why doctors, like the two on this Committee, who are accustomed in their consulting rooms to hearing the truth about sexuality, and gaining scientific knowledge of its various manifestations, should move so far towards conciliating the superego representatives by whom they were heavily outnumbered. Perhaps it is only the analyst, who has had his knowledge of the instinct reservoir of the id and the vicissitudes of the libido thoroughly engrained, who can be relied upon to resist the folly of pretence and not be taken in by 'respectability'. I may add, however, that even the analyst's knowledge is superficial, relevant to his engrained and indoctrinated reactive patterns of his earlier life, and it is not impossible for him too to succumb in a very legal atmosphere to feeling that nature is sinful and wicked.

There are other reactive patterns with which we are less familiar, and which therefore may strike us as so very odd when we encounter them in our work. I was consulted by a man whom I shall describe as qualifying, on superficial manifestations, for the late Dr Kinsey's number four or five hetero-homosexual rating. He was a great big powerful fellow. He alleged that he had enough heterosexuality in him to justify his hope of being cured of his homosexual tendencies. The evidence for this was that he had on several occasions performed the heterosexual act successfully, and had for a time even lived with a woman with some degree of sexual relationship. At one of his early sessions he told me that he had a confession to make; he had been so emotionally worked up by the music of an opera that he had left the opera-house, gone to a nearby railway station and looked for a man. In a few minutes his solicitations were successful; but walking home with the man, he decided that he did not like him, and so said goodbye and went back to the station, where he found another unknown man with whom everything went successfully.

I had already begun to feel that this practising homosexual was a poor bid for analytical success, and therefore, most unanalytically, I taxed him with the question: 'You come here allegedly to be cured of your homosexuality, to become hetero-sexual, and yet even while under treatment, when your sexual feelings are aroused (by the music), you leave the opera and look for a *man*. In the circumstances, if you had to look for a sexual partner, why on earth didn't you look for a woman?'

This huge man rolled over on to his side, half sat up and stared me in the face: 'Good heavens!' he said, 'I had never thought of that. Good heavens! Pick up a woman? Why, I wouldn't have a clue!'

Thus it may be recognized that what to the heterosexual man may present little difficulty, namely that of making the acquaintance of an unknown woman, or easier still perhaps, picking up a prostitute, had no pattern in this homosexual's psyche. It seems to me that one might have asked the average heterosexual man to go to a railway station and 'pick up' an unknown *man*. What he probably would pick up would be a plain-clothes detective, with the well-known results! And perhaps the exceptional cases to which fate is so unkind are the less homosexual

41

ones. These libidinal relationships between persons are obviously something which emanates from deeper unconscious emotional or instinctual sources, and cannot be taken over by the ego at anyone's command. All that the ego can do is to sit in judgment over them, and dole out punishment.

Now perhaps I ought to ask myself why it is that in reading this beautifully worded and beautifully reasoned report, *my* first emotional reaction is one of indignation and contempt. I think the answer, or one of the answers, may well be this: throughout one's many years of training analysis (for which daily attendance used to be required) one was encouraged in exposing to consciousness proclivities in oneself similar to those exhibited by these gentlemen and ladies of the Wolfenden Committee. One's object was to analyze these proclivities, to trace them to their source and to see how they were made. Quite early one began to discover that these were an enormous defensive construction designed to defend our socially timid and highly susceptible consciousness from a recognition of the, at that time, intolerable truths that dwelt without our unconscious minds, and the unconscious minds of all other persons. Indeed, that is the very source of everything that goes on in us, positive and negative, expressive, prohibitive and defensive. It is only by virtue of years of this self-examination that one qualifies to become an analyst, to be in a position to understand the perplexities in the minds of others.

And now in this year of grace, one meets a representative body of the educated public, who appear to be not even aware of the need, or possibility of the existence, source or mechanisms of these very phenomena which it has been assigned to examine, to pass judgment upon and to make recommendations! The members of this body proceed to struggle with their assignment, their task, from this position of abysmal ignorance. The analyst can see that, like all their beliefs and behaviours, these deliberations and expressions of theirs are determined by conflict, conflict in which, if the superego does not have supreme command behaviouristically, it can at least pretend to such command and allege its omnipotence. Parent images, now represented by society, would tolerate nothing less.

The Report opens with the announcement 'we were appointed on 24th August 1954', and having read the Report, I am inclined to remark that they do not mention whether it was A.D. or B.C.! It was certainly before psychology or psychoanalysis had been dreamed of, at any rate by them. One could almost imagine the primal horde father arriving on the scene and subjecting all the weaker males to general castration all round. This is not so fantastic as it sounds, for in the primitive life of today, more conspicuously amongst primitive tribes, but also in the primitive life within civilization (relics of the past), this is what the older generation is doing to the younger, though it is commonly called a 'circumcision' rather than a 'castration' rite, and tends to become less physical and more mental as civilization advances. Patients have described to me how their long years of education at public schools and so forth, and the general indoctrination accompanying it, was felt by them to be a protracted 'castration'. And so it will come out even in the Wolfenden Report!

Not the least of the dangers of this Report is the fact that it is so plausibly and reasonably written. I am a little tempted here to quote several paragraphs to illustrate what I mean by this smooth reasonableness. It tends to lead the reader away or astray from intellectually less satisfying truths, but perhaps I can illustrate what I mean, though not nearly so satisfactorily, by taking a few random excerpts from a succession of sections and leaving the rest to the reader's imagination.

Paragraph 66 : 'It seems to us that there are four sets of considerations which should govern the decision on this point (the age at which a man is regarded as an adult). The first is connected with the need to protect young and immature persons; the second is connected with the age at which the pattern of a man's sexual development can be said to be fixed; the third is connected with the meaning of the word 'adult' in the sense of 'responsible for his own actions'; and the fourth is connected with the consequences which would follow from the fixing of any particular age . . . '

Paragraph 67 : 'So far as concerns the first set of considerations, we have made it clear throughout our report that we recognize the need for protecting the young and immature . . . and we find it hard to believe that he needs to be protected from would-be seducers more carefully than a girl does . . . On this view, there would be some ground for making sixteen the age of 'adulthood', since sexual intercourse with a willing girl of this age is not unlawful.'

Paragraph 68 : 'We have given special attention to the evidence which has been given to us in connection with the second set of considerations—those which relate the notion of "adulthood" to a recognizable age in the fixation of a young man's sexual pattern—for we should not wish to see legalised, etc. etc. etc. . . . Our medical witnesses were unanimously of the view that the main sexual pattern is laid down in the early years of life, and the majority of them held that it was usually fixed, in main outline, by the age of sixteen. Many hold that it was fixed much earlier . . . '

Paragraph 70 : 'To suggest that the age of adulthood for the purposes we have in mind should be twenty-one leads us to the fourth set of considerations we have mentioned, namely, the consequences which would follow from the decision about any particular age. To fix the age at twenty-one (or indeed at any age above seventeen) raises particular difficulties in this connection, for it involves leaving liable to prosecution a young man of almost twenty-one for actions which in a few days' time he could perform without breaking the law. This difficulty would admittedly arise whatever age was decided upon, for it would always be the case that an action would be illegal a few days below that age and legal above it. But this difficulty would present itself in a less acute form if the age were fixed at eighteen, which is the other age most frequently suggested to us. For whereas it would be difficult to regard a young man of nearly twenty-one charged with a homosexual offence as a suitable subject for "care or protection" under the provisions of the Children and Young Persons Acts, it would not be entirely inappropriate so to regard a youth under eighteen. If the age of adulthood for the purposes of our amendment were fixed at eighteen, and if the "care or protection" provisions were extended to cover young persons up to that age, there would be a means of dealing with homosexual behaviour by those under that age without invoking the penal sanctions of the criminal law.' Finally the age decided upon was twenty-one.

If one reads page after page of this sort of verbiage, one is apt to be lulled into a more or less acquiescent state of mind, and to forget that it is mostly a series of platitudes chosen arbitrarily for the sake of arriving at decisions, worked over and through and through with so much obsessional examination and re-examination that we gain the impression that everything possible has been taken into consideration, no detail has been left out, nobody could contribute any further item to the discussion, and therefore the conclusions and recommendations framed so smoothly and with such an illusion of reasonableness must be the ultimate truth. Perhaps they are the ultimate truth if the truth is debarred from entering consciousness, and that is the indoctrination which protects the average person from realising unwanted truths about himself and others. Perhaps we have to go round and round in repetitive obsessional circles of deliberations, but we must ensure that we do not get anywhere near knowing what we must not know, that would disturb our equilibrium. Perhaps we find it less anxiety-provoking to be an animal on the one hand and pretend to be a god on the other. We hope to convince everybody to our own advantage and we may even convince ourselves, and how satisfactory it all is!

On the other hand scientific, especially psychoanalytic investigation of the phenomenon of homosexuality is not concerned with these plausible coverings up and attendant self-satisfactions. It is concerned with finding out the causes and psychopathology of the condition, in spite of the resistances in the mind to allowing these to enter consciousness. Therefore, like all science, its theories have progressed through a succession of stages. Originally homosexuality was connected specifically with aberrations of the Oedipus complex, and there is no doubt that this is true so far as it goes. We see the patient, whose clinical material reveals that he has identified himself with his mother in an attempt to escape the awful consequences of father-rivalry, and so on. But in recent years some of the very modern analysts claim to have traced the aetiology of homosexuality right back to a pre-Oedipus level. In doing so they already had a guide from Freud, for in 1910, writing of Leonardo da Vinci, he said: 'We will for the moment leave aside the question as to what connection there is between homosexuality and sucking at the mother's breast.' Many homosexuals show on the auto-erotic plane oral fixation and on the object-relationship plane, mother or breast-nipple fixation.

Many years later, Freud declared that 'the child discovers the pleasure-giving genital zone—penis or clitoris—during sucking. I shall leave it undecided whether the child really takes this newly-acquired source of pleasure as a substitute for the recently lost nipple of the mother's breast.'

It has been pointed out that even the homosexual, in common with everybody, had a first and therefore most important experience in life at his mother's breast, or with his mother. Such a first experience must be incorporated into his homosexual phantasies and feelings and activities. It would seem that he has abandoned his mother's breast or nipple by displacement of the affects associated with it, on to the male organs. There is little doubt that this transfer or displacement is attained via the individual's own body, via his own penis, and this has everything to do with the familiar narcissism of the homosexual. He has the whole thing with him, in his person, all the valuable objects, including the first one, his mother's breast or nipple.

One of my homosexual patients, a highly educated and cultured man, who, by the way, did not practise homosexuality, in the course of his analysis related the following very apposite story: he was his mother's darling and as an infant had never been separated from her. Then on his fifth birthday, he remembers the date because it was his fifth birthday, he got scarlet fever. In those days it was compulsory that scarlet fever cases be removed to the fever hospital, and so it came about that that night he found himself disconsolate in a hospital bed, without his mother. He was heartbroken and felt he would die of misery. Then, having nothing to do, he started moving his hands about his body. (I expect he was searching for his mother's nipple.) Low down on his abdomen he suddenly came across a spot the sensations from which electrified him. He had found his glans penis. He masturbated for the first time in his life and felt that all was well, and he hardly needed mother any more.

It would seem possible that the homosexual who has orally regressed to the nipple level, perhaps out of some disappointment or imagined let-down by the mother, has unconsciously substituted penis excitement (originally in himself) for the first and greatest pleasure in life at the mother's breast. For a time this valuable source of satisfaction (his penis) remains with him and is responsible for the well-known 'penis-pride' of the boy, but subsequently displacement takes place on to other objects who, like himself, are endowed with this stimulating anatomical structure. Of course other readjustments of the psychic economy take place, including a repudiation of everything feminine and an increasing canalization of all sexual potentialities on to this 'new'-found form of enjoying the old, repressed and forgotten situation.

After this brief itemized excursion into the realms of psycho-pathology, can we force ourselves to come back to the Wolfenden Report, with its recommendations based upon newly acquired, superficial 'knowledge' of the manifestations of homo-sexuality? Unfortunately people who are not fortified with a background of deep psychopathological knowledge, are apt to forget this and transgress into remarks and recommendations which would be possible only out of ignorance. For instance, in para. 200 the Report says: 'A prison sentence can, in many cases, detrimentally affect any prospect of successful treatment, so that the offender remains in a state of mind predisposed to the repetition of his offence.'

If the members of the Committee really recognize this truth, surely it is incongruous of them in the face of it to support and even to increase penalties of long terms of imprisonment. One may wonder how many conflicting motives are at work in their discussions and recommendations. They go on to say: 'If, by the use of other methods, the offender can be successfully brought to a state of better adjustment to society in which he is less disposed to repeat his offence, then clearly society gains. The Cambridge survey, however, shows that the proportion of homosexual offenders subsequently reconvicted was almost the same in the case of offenders who had been placed on probation (29·9 per cent) as it was in the case of offenders who had been sent to prison (30·1 per cent).'

I am glad they make this last confession, because in their deliberations they more or less give the impression that they are the non-sinners holding out a hand to the sinners, and actually use such words as rehabilitation, better integration with social life, higher ideals, a greater degree of sublimation, and so forth. I wondered how they would put this across to such people as Leonardo da Vinci, Julius Caesar, and in modern times the vast number of eminent men whose names of course cannot be mentioned. Naturally the homosexual is not necessarily

FEAR, PUNISHMENT, ANXIETY

endowed with greater insight into the psychopathology of homosexuality or of heterosexuality than is the average person, but in the light of what we know of psychology, this does not warrant the heterosexual feeling superior to the homosexual, or regarding him as somebody to whom he can teach better ways.

It occurred to me in reading certain conclusions of the Report, that like the Wolfenden Committee, we are all (or most of us) in one camp, and therefore apt to feel how reasonable is everything the Committee says, or rather we jump from one camp to another leaving all knowledge of our previous camp out of consciousness, and putting up barriers against its re-entry. Therefore I tentatively tried the effect of one rather unselected paragraph of the Report upon a mature homosexual, and fairly intelligent, man patient. I told him to interrupt me with any remark that he felt like making. Rather arbitrarily I chose para. 196: 'From whichever of the foregoing points of view it may be regarded, treatment itself will vary through a wide range, if only to match the diversity of individual personalities.' At this point the patient expostulated sarcastically: '*Sic*.' 'It is important to remember that "treatment need not necessarily, or even often, imply any active steps to be taken by a physician or by a psychiatrist. Often it will be desirable that various methods of treatment should be applied simultaneously, bringing into service a combination of many helpers.'

At this point the patient laughed and added: 'Uncle Tom Cobley and all.' Later, where the term 'Successful results' is used, the patient remarked: 'It is all lies, the only successful result is not being caught, and naturally one tells any lies to assist that.'

Having been loosened up, this patient went on to say: 'I wish they would set up a committee of homosexuals to say what they think of *heterosexuality*. I will tell you this much: most of us think it is absolutely disgusting. We cannot understand why anybody wants to behave like that. Perhaps it would be a good thing if the penalties they inflict on us were inflicted on them instead!' These remarks are of course in keeping with the attitude that the only important reality matter is not to be caught. But if we compromise between the two points of view, perhaps we could wash them both out and suggest that the law should, as it generally attempts to do (I hope), be concerned merely with the protection of the public against unwanted interference.

I think it may be said for the Wolfenden Committee that had their terms of reference been limited to a consideration of the law and practice relating to homosexual offences, they may have had at least some firm ground to stand on, and may not have done so badly. It seems to me that it has been the additional and perhaps unjustified matter of considering the *treatment* of homosexual offenders that has got them embroiled into very complicated matters far out of their depth. In fact, it has forced them to encroach upon the province of a science of which they knew nothing.

More than this, it has stimulated and to some extent revealed to us the enormous defensive construction built up against the repressed bogies in the mind, not a suitable basis for dispassionate or scientific research. The first research, as is the case in every individual analysis, has to be directed against this defensive construction, for it is only from beneath this that the unconscious phantasies which are the source of all our behaviours and beliefs, can be admitted to consciousness. Perhaps this Report is a good lesson in the futility of trying to unravel and assess psychological phenomena without first removing the obstacles to understanding their meaning.

The Wolfenden Committee evidently preferred to listen to policemen as a basis on which to judge not only homosexual crimes but homosexuality. As regards their assignment relating to crime there is some justification but to my mind crime is crime and is not necessarily anything to do with homosexuality. We cannot be too clear in our minds in distinguishing between crime and psychopathology. Crime involves violation of other people's freedom and liberty (the sort of thing we tend to do to homosexuals just because they are homosexuals). Crime has not necessarily anything to do with homosexuality, but operates in every field of human activity, but it would seem that we tend to lose our reason when it comes to homosexuality, on account of our emotionally overcharged repressed conflicts. This comes out clearly in the disproportionate severity of the legal penalties.

When it comes to the second assignment of the Committee, namely the practice relating to 'the treatment of persons convicted of such (homosexual) offences', I would suggest that the Committee would have done better to read Freud than to listen

to policemen. Had they done so they might have come across the following letter which, written in the 1930's, reveals far greater enlightenment than anything which they have to offer us. It was sent to a despairing mother in America, who had written to ask advice about her son. This is the first paragraph:
'I gather from your letter that your son is a homosexual. I am most impressed by the fact that you do not mention this term yourself in your information about him. May I question you, why you avoid it? Homosexuality is assuredly no advantage, but it is nothing to be ashamed of, no vice, no degradation, it cannot be classified as an illness; we consider it to be a variation of the sexual function produced by a certain arrest of sexual development. Many highly respected individuals of ancient and modern times have been homosexuals, several of the greatest men among them (Plato, Michelangelo, Leonardo da Vinci, etc.). It is a great injustice to persecute homosexuality as a crime, and cruelty too . . . '[1]

It strikes one that had the Wolfenden Committee read Freud, even up to 1930, they might have saved themselves three years of perplexity and trouble and the nation £8,046 (the estimated cost of preparing the Report) . . . and what is of course more important than any of this, arrived at an enlightened conclusion.

[1] Volume III of *Sigmund Freud—The Last Phase, 1919-1939*, by Ernest Jones.

II

The Psychology of Punishment

In recent years it has been pointed out that delinquent and criminal behaviour is commonly motivated by unconscious forces and is, therefore, not a product of the ego or reason. In consequence, attempts to prevent and to rectify such behaviour by measures such as punishment directed solely towards the ego are doomed to failure because they leave its unconscious sources unaffected. In fact, it was probably repeated failures (a large number of criminals are punished again and again without effect) that finally led the jurist to pay a little attention, however reluctantly, to the psychological point of view. That this attention should be so little, and that it should be so reluctantly given, are evidences which contribute to the conclusion—the main theme of this paper—that the behaviour of the punisher, like that of his opposite number, the punished, is not free from contributions from an unconscious or non-ego level of the mind.

This paper proposes to show that, like delinquency, the compulsion to punish delinquency has its origins in similar unconscious or emotional levels—that, like delinquency, it is more a product of instinct and emotion than of reason. Thus the punisher would appear to be the victim of unconscious forces and mechanisms similar to those of the punished and, therefore, a most unsuitable person to treat the latter's symptoms. His complete failure to effect a cure, or indeed to throw any light upon the disease, tends to confirm this conclusion.

It will hardly be claimed that there is *no* difference between the punisher and the punished, between the criminal and the jurist. Their position sociologically is a very different one, and this must be brought about by differences in their psychology. One's position is very different according to which side one takes in a civil war. If the emotional values are not too strong in proportion to the ego values, the sane person—that is, the person with the relatively greater ability to conform to his ego values—will choose the winning side. Thus we may conclude that the punisher has more capacity for ego valuation, is more sane than the punished. If he is similarly driven by his unconscious emotional needs, he is getting his relief or gratification, at least in greater conformity with his ego requirements. Admittedly there is an ego difference between the punisher and the punished. There is also frequently, though not invariably, a deeper non-ego difference. The punished is frequently unconsciously in need of punishment while the punisher is unconsciously in need of inflicting it. There is a difference therefore in the balance of the emotional conflict. There is a difference between masochism and sadism, though a difference which is more apparent than real, as is evidenced by their reversibility. The ego has to do merely with the execution of the act which gives release to the tension.

Lest it should be thought that the importance of the ego in the institution of punishment is being underestimated, and as a preliminary to exposing the mental forces and mechanisms at work, it is necessary to review samples of the sociological data. These will include a few legal punishments past and present, a brief review of the principle or theory of punishment as advanced by jurists and others, evidence of the psychology of some criminals, and finally a clinical case history showing in operation the various forces which produce the need to punish. This last is the special evidence which justifies the writing of this paper. If this and the conclusions drawn from it seem unduly deferred, delay may be justified by the greater comprehensiveness in data and the greater conviction in results. In the meantime there is much relevant matter of interest to be considered.

2. HISTORICAL SURVEY

Without a study of evolution, life as it exists today would be imperfectly understood, and without some chronological survey, legal punishment of today would lack its true perspective.

Nevertheless, it is necessary to emphasize that the subject of this paper is the psychology of punishment and not the history of punishment. Naturally, therefore, material which is irrelevant to a clear insight into this psychology is excluded no matter how relevant it may be to a comprehensive historical review.

For instance, I am fully aware that large numbers of reformers have fought for generations to modify the more obvious sadism of our legal practices. Beccaria, Penn, Howard, Fry, Romilly, Bentham, Gall, Franklin, Montaigne, Moore, Fielding, Dickens, Shaw, Galsworthy, Tolstoi, Dostoevsky, Voltaire, Victor Hugo, Zola, Melville, Dreiser, Gollancz, Silverman and a host of unnamed and unnameable reformers and writers have all contributed the modifying influence of enlightenment and of reason to the unthinking emotional reaction, the naïve sadism of public, jurist and ecclesiastic.

Their arguments, theories and activities, though most relevant to a paper on the history of punishment or to a paper on the psychology of *opposition* to punishment, do not help to elucidate the deeper psychopathology of punishment, its advocacy, institution and maintenance. Perhaps, therefore, there is no need to apologize for their omission from the following abbreviated review.

From the earliest times of which there is any record, crimes were not judged by utilitarian standards but by the supposed offence given to some tribal deity.[1] If the tribe did not punish the culprit, the outraged god would punish the whole tribe with a terrible vengeance (e.g. the story of Jonah). Thus it was believed that incest would anger the gods and bring down their curse on the crops.[2]

The types of punishment inflicted were almost invariably castration equivalents.[3] The Chinese Book of Rites, which goes back to Confucius (500 B.C.) names four punishments: branding, cutting off the nose, cutting off the feet, and death.

---

[1] The present-day legal attitude towards acts of sexual perversion that do not infringe the liberty of the person and towards bestiality may fairly be taken as the true successors of the above attitude. The standard is not utilitarian, and the impression is that a psychological equivalent of the tribal deity is implied if not avowed.

[2] Fraser, *Golden Bough.*

[3] Melanie Klein (*The Psychoanalysis of Children*, 1932) tells us that: 'Children who, unconsciously, were expecting to be cut to pieces, beheaded, devoured and so on, would feel compelled to be naughty and to get punished.' 'Castration' might well be included here. Alternatively, they would doubtless develop a sadistic superego, equivalent in violence to the instinct urges it was meant to oppose (anti-cathexis). This is the sort of thing that happens in obsessional neurosis. Freud has said that without exception these are persons who, even in early life, betrayed their unconscious aggressiveness.

Punishment, if not actually partaken in by the public, was at least a much-appreciated public spectacle. With the attainment of a higher degree of civilization the art of showmanship advanced and punishment as an enjoyable entertainment became an important part of civic life. This was notably the case in Rome, where the Roman holiday, in addition to the arena practice of throwing criminals to wild animals, included many variations, such as the public castration of minor offenders.

It cannot be denied that there was overt sadistic enjoyment in the infliction of punishment during the childhood of civilization. In the exercise of this violent superego activity, those very urges which were being punished, namely, the aggressive and the libidinal (in short, the sadistic), were evidently much exercised and enjoyed. The urge to punish is thus seen to derive its dynamic force from those very instincts which it proposed to destroy. It is therefore merely another mode of expressing and enjoying those instincts. The particular mechanism employed is almost identical with that of neurosis where the instinct is gratified and the superego opposition is expressed in one and the same symptomatic act. The only essential difference is that in the case of punishment it is the criminal and not one's own instinct or id that is identified with the fantasied bad object. By virtue of this projection the punisher may now identify himself with the superego and freely enjoy the release of his instinct-derived impulses at the expense of a scapegoat; the 'neurosis' is now extra-psychic—in the outer world—instead of being intra-psychic.

The character of punishment as here portrayed has remained consistent throughout the ages. Its sadistic nature and the overt enjoyment of it by punishers and public, have shown no important changes until quite recent times. In England, in the Saxon period, mutilation was still the favourite punishment.[1] Eyes, tongues and scalps were torn away. In the Norman period, hunting in the king's preserves was punished by castration.[2] (It is interesting here to remember the equivalent in the unconscious.) It was common to cut off the right hand at the same time. Flogging was often carried to unbelievable lengths. In 1530 an Act

[1] Parry, *History of Torture in England* (London).

[2] Home, *History of London.*

54

was passed to deal with vagabonds, as follows: 'Such idle person shall be had to the next market town tied to the end of a cart, naked, and beaten with whips throughout the town until his body be bloody by reason of such whipping.'

Titus Oates, twice flogged through London, is said to have received over two thousand lashes. The intention was to flog him to death (cf. the impulse in the clinical case recorded in V), but he survived.

The following is an instance of a death sentence pronounced by a judge in the reign of Queen Elizabeth: 'Thou shalt be drawn through the open City of London to the place of execution and there hanged and let down alive, and thy privy parts cut off and thy entrails taken out and burned in thy sight. Then thy head shall be cut off and thy body divided into four parts to be disposed of at Her Majesty's pleasure; and God have mercy on thy soul.'

If one reads accounts of the excitement and the drunken revelry in and about Newgate and all along the route from there to Tyburn (as late as the nineteenth century) one can have no doubt that punishment was a great emotional outlet. As at the ancient Roman arena the space at Tyburn Tree (Marble Arch) was provided with seats for which a fee was charged. In the seventeenth century, animals, corpses, and children were solemnly tried and executed. As late as 1801 a boy of twelve was strung up by the public hangman for the theft of a spoon from a dwelling house.

Overt savagery in punishment was slow to die in spite of the efforts of many reformers. It is not unusual even today to hear magistrates and others expressing regret at the mitigation of the general resort to birchings and other forms of violence. And this in spite of all the teachings of reformers. As long ago as 1764 Beccaria detected an implicit relationship between the psychology of crime and punishment when he wrote: 'The countries most noted for the severity of punishments were always those in which the most bloody and inhuman actions were committed, for the hand of the assassin and the legislator were directed by the same spirit of ferocity.'[1]

---

[1] Beccaria, *Dei delitti e delle pene,* quoted by Wilson in *The Crime of Punishment,* p. 147.

He was followed by Bentham who said: 'Be slow to believe in death. By disusing it as a punishment you will prevent it as a crime.'[1] And by Romilly: 'Cruel punishments have an inevitable tendency to produce cruelty in a people.'[2]

Thackeray, at the conclusion of a description of an execution he saw in 1840, wrote: ' . . . I came away that morning with a disgust for murder; but it was for *the murder I saw done* . . . '[3]

Nevertheless, where customs, well or badly rationalized, have their source in instinctual gratification, the public is loth to forego them.

If punishments in general emphasise the aggressive component of the sadistic impulse (masquerading as superego), a study of the centuries of the witch epidemic (1484-1793) provide us with ample material emphasizing the libidinal component. For example, the Hopkins test consisted of thrusting long pins or bodkins (especially made for the purpose) into various parts of the accused woman's naked body. If at any moment the victim did not cry out with pain, the 'witch's mark' was said to have been found and guilt established. Wickwar says: 'When one considers that the torture was carried on until there was probably an insensibility to all feeling, it is easy to imagine that the witch-finder always scored.' 'In the Malleus these matters (ideas of fornication with the Devil, etc.) are argued to the finest point of sophistry, and the rules laid down are of such a nature as to prevent the escape from horrible torture or death of any woman that might be accused by a spiteful neighbour.'[4]

The impression conveyed by these and other records of punishments is that the mechanism of transferring the sadistic impulses to the service of the superego facilitates social organization and enables them to achieve a new lease of life and freedom.

A few statistics may lend point to this contention. In Europe the total number of victims ran well into millions.[5] In Spain, in the brief period of eighteen years of his administration (1481-99), Torquemada alone burnt at the stake or otherwise had done to death 105,294 persons.[6] During the sixteenth and seventeenth

---

[1] Bentham quoted by Wilson in *The Crime of Punishment*, p. 151.
[2] Romilly, *ibid*. p. 165.
[3] Thackeray, *ibid*. p. 171.
[4] Ernest Jones, *On the Nightmare*, p. 223.
[5] W. G. Soldan, *Geschichte der Hexenprozesse*, 1880 edition, 1, 181.
[6] Llorente, *History of the Inquisition*, p. 578.

centuries of the Spanish Inquisition the population of that country was appreciably lowered, falling from twenty million to six million. 'Although the actual extent of the epidemic may have been exaggerated by some writers, nothing can exaggerate the horror of the detailed cruelty.'[1]

It is difficult to believe that any amount of private infliction of torture and murder would ever reach commensurate figures. The only comparable depletion of a population by human action would be due to war, another superego organisation of the aggressive and libidinal urges on a national scale.

Enough has been said to indicate that punishment included in its source and early practice those very instincts, aggressive and libidinal, which it professed to repudiate and destroy.

It might be assumed that the modifications of punishment which have since taken place, particularly the much later development of imprisonment as a punishment, must be an indication of the ego having taken the matter in hand. It might be thought that punishment was a sadistic enjoyment, but now is a product of reality considerations and of reason—that its psychology has changed. Apart from the fact that no new principle or theory has been advocated, such alteration is not necessarily the case. In the light of evolution it would appear almost miraculous if such a revolutionary change had in fact taken place. The same *principle,* that of punishment, has been, and is still being, maintained, and it seems likely that quite other elements than those of science or reality are responsible for the apparent changes in practice. For instance, it might be assumed that the cessation of such a fantastic procedure as the torture and burning of women for fornication with the devil must have been the product of a saner psychology. After a profound study of the subject, Ernest Jones came to a very different conclusion: 'The end of the Witch epidemic needs almost as much explanation as its origin . . . There was a notable increase in Puritanism . . . the general attitude towards sex and sexuality underwent a very extensive change. Instead of its being loudly declaimed and stamped on as a dangerous sin, it became more and more suppressed as a topic of public discussion. . . . Now this change of attitude was quite inconsistent with a continuance

[1] Ernest Jones, *On the Nightmare,* p. 224.

of the Witch epidemic, for the Witch trials consisted largely of ventilating in great detail the most repellant aspects of sexuality. . . . The very factor, therefore, namely excessive sexual repression, that had made the Witchcraft epidemic possible in the first place, was, when developed to a more intense degree, an important one in destroying its own fruit. We are familiar with clinical parallels to this process; many neurotic manifestations of a given stage of repression become incompatible with a more intense one, the erotic source of them being intolerable, and so disappear.'[1] Thus Ernest Jones concludes that witch trials disappeared, *not* on account of sanity prevailing over the disease, but, on the contrary, on account of the disease process progressing to a further and more severe stage.

We may ask if it may not be on account of further repression that we have hidden our injuries of accused persons behind prison walls. May this be the modern equivalent of that earlier repression of the sadism of punishment which found its expression in the Eastern habit of burying alive? Barnes says: 'The cruelties of present-day imprisonment are for the most part screened from the specific knowledge of the public. . . . The key to the defects, abuses and cruelties of the present prison system is to be found in the fact that, whatever the pretext, the actual purpose of imprisonment is not reformation but punishment. Of course, the older attitude of conventional penology was that punishment itself necessarily produces reformation, but we now know that in most cases exactly the opposite result is brought about.'[2] (Vide III of this paper.)

We may reflect that it was not so very long ago that the manifestly insane were similarly manacled and chained and subjected to *punitive* detention. May it not be that this is still, though less manifestly, the case? On the basis of laboriously compiled statistics comparing the countries of Europe and elsewhere in the ratio of members of asylums to the number of prison inmates, Penrose concludes that: 'as a general rule, if the prison services are extensive, the asylum population is relatively small and the reverse also tends to be true'.[3]

Further, with reference to prison population he says: 'It may

[1] *Ibid.* pp. 228 et seq.
[2] Barnes, *Repression of Crime*, p. 289.
[3] Penrose in *Brit. J. Med. Psychol.*, 18, 1.

be that the first attempt at controlling these people is to provide prisons with a view to punishing them in the hope that they will ultimately be made into good citizens. Thus, the community first evolves a system of jurisdiction supported by prisons: later on, the medico-psychological attitude towards crime develops and the people who, in earlier epochs, would have been confined in prison become subjects for medical investigation and treatment. This view received some support from the history of the treatment of criminals in a given country, such as England: indeed, in the earliest asylums, patients were often confined, like prisoners, in chains.'[1]

It would seem, according to Barnes, that if prisoners are not at first 'subjects for medical investigation and treatment' they bid fair to become so: 'Particularly serious, though almost uniformly overlooked, is the total denial of any sex life to all the inmates of penal institutions, in spite of the fact that many prisoners are of a hyper-sexed type who have been leading an unusually free sex life before incarceration.'[2] It may be that this would not be so injurious in itself if there were adequate opportunity for displacement and sublimation of the suppressed sex instincts through professional, cultural and recreational outlets.'[3] What may be 'serious' is that not only are the instincts suppressed but also their natural displacements and sublimations are denied. If this is not inconsistent with mental health, it is certainly putting a burden upon the mind's natural tendency to find healthy adjustment.

Evidence of this state of affairs is shown in prisons by the way the sex urge seeks, and often finds, expression in all sorts of pathological conduct. Barnes says: 'If one were to plan an institution designed to promote sexual degeneracy one would arrive at the modern prison.'[4] We may reflect that this sexual degeneracy is just an attempt on the part of the psyche to find an outlet for mental tension which would otherwise further damage it, perhaps to the extent of a permanent psychosis.

I have been told by an ex-prisoner that the above is true of some prisons, particularly of convict prisons, but not of others.

[1] *Ibid.* p. 8.
[2] Barnes, *Repression of Crime*, p. 289.
[3] *Ibid.* p. 292.
[4] *Ibid.* p. 292.

In these others, according to him, his main preoccupation was hunger: 'For two years, during every part of my waking life, I was never free from the consciousness of hunger.' How much of this may have been a displacement of sexual hunger I do not know. If it had objective causes, the question arises whether it is any less injurious to the psyche than protracted sexual hunger.

To assess the degree of injury suffered by legal punishment of whatever degree or variety it would be necessary to conduct a clinical study of individual cases—perhaps a further extension of the sort of work done by Dr Palthorpe in her book, *What we put in Prison*. Such a study would bring us to the conclusion that punishment implies injury, physical or mental, to its victim. I hope to show later on that it provides, at the same time, a certain satisfaction or helpful outlet for those employing this mode of relief.

To lend emphasis to the very practical contention that the psychology of punishment has not altered in its fundamental character, I am tempted to draw a comparison between the legal sadism of the sixteenth century and that of modern times by recording a specimen of the descriptions of punishment which abound in every book on its history, and then to follow this by an excerpt, chosen at random, from a newspaper description of a very recent Court scene.

The following account is chosen from Mr. Lytton Strachey's *Elizabeth and Essex,* in which he says at that time it was practically impossible for anyone accused of treason to be acquitted. The accused were Dr Lopez, Physician in Chief to Queen Elizabeth, and with him a fellow-Portuguese and a young Spanish soldier.

'Then—it was June 1594—the three men, bound to hurdles, were dragged up Holborn, past the doctor's house, to Tyburn. A vast crowd was assembled to enjoy the spectacle. The doctor, standing on the scaffold, attempted in vain to make a dying speech; the mob . . . howled with laughter. . . . He was strung up and—such was the routine of the law—cut down while life was still in him. Then the rest of the time-honoured punishment —castration, disembowelling and quartering—was carried out. Ferreira was the next to suffer. After that, it was the turn of Tinoco. He had seen what was to be his fate, twice repeated, and close enough. His ears were filled with the shrieks and moans of his companions, and his eyes with every detail of the contortions and the blood. . . . Tinoco, cut down too soon, recovered his feet after the hanging. He was lusty and desperate; and he fell upon his executioners. The crowd, wild with excitement . . . broke through the guards . . . but before long, the instincts of law and order reasserted themselves. Two stalwart fellows, seeing that the executioner was giving ground, rushed forward to his rescue. Tinoco was felled by a blow on the head; he was held firmly down on the scaffold; and like the others, castrated, disembowelled, and quartered.'

In November 1942 at Newport Assizes thirteen men were sentenced for mutual homosexual offences. The police admitted that all but one of the men were of a 'certain type', that is to say, were homosexual psychopaths and were probably already suffering mentally. They received sentences varying from ten years' penal servitude to twelve months' imprisonment and totalling fifty-seven years between them. Two of the men had made determined attempts to commit suicide. One who had taken rat poison left a note saying, 'I cannot stand the scandal. That has always been my trouble. I have no guts.' A fourteenth, a youth of nineteen, who should have stood his trial with them, had already committed suicide. The first man to be sentenced (to ten years' penal servitude) fainted and had to be carried from the dock.

This excerpt from a newspaper is incomplete, but may suffice to indicate that though the sadism of the modern criminal trial can hardly be said to equal Renaissance torture in its vividness, nevertheless, individual suffering is comparable.

Bernard Shaw says: 'Imprisonment, as it exists today, is a worse crime than any of those committed by its victims; for no single criminal can be as powerful for evil, or as unrestrained in its exercise, as an organized nation. . . . To punish is to injure, to reform is to heal; you cannot mend a person by damaging him.'[1]

In conclusion, the psychology of punishment may be tentatively divided into three stages. The first stage may be called the pre-punishment stage and regarded as the free expression of the instincts of aggressiveness and sexuality, either singly or

---

[1] Bernard Shaw: Preface to Webb, *English Prisons under Local Government*.

combined as sadism, together with the retaliatory reaction of their victim.

The second stage arises as a result of repression of the first. In consequence of this repression the instincts are anti-cathected, and obtain their outlet as superego activities—naturally directed against their original form. This last is projected on to a scapegoat and the sadistic activity is then freely and openly enjoyed at his expense.

The third stage is a result of a further degree of repression (cf. Ernest Jones's explanation of the cessation of witch trials). The disease has progressed further so that now the open expression of sadism, even in the form of punishment, can no longer be tolerated. It becomes repressed into the unconscious, and its victim becomes similarly hidden behind the prison walls. Inside the prison—the objective equivalent of the unconscious— the same process goes on unseen by consciousness and inaccessible to ego-interference.

3. OLD THEORIES OF PUNISHMENT

The old theories advanced to explain the phenomenon of legal punishment are obviously rationalizations and do not merit detailed consideration. We have space to select only a few typical examples, and to subject them merely to a very brief review.

The Prison Commissioners, under the long Chairmanship of Sir E. Ruggles-Brise—it lasted from 1895 to 1920—evidently felt that their duty was to justify the existing order. They tried to combine all theories and principles in the supreme object— punishment. 'Prisons exist for punishment,' they said. The chief principles involved in punishment were said to be:

(1) Retribution
(2) Deterrence
(3) Reform

To take these in order:

Retribution

The then Archbishop of York, in the role of penal reformer, made the following public statement: 'The first duty of the State is to dissociate itself from the act of its own member; to do this it must act, not only upon but against that member. . .

His act implicates the community, unless the community repudiates it. The community must exhibit an antagonism in its will against the will of the offending member. This is necessary for the preservation of its own character on which the character of its citizens largely depends.'[1]

It would appear from this that it is necessary for us to emphasize by retributive punishment that we, for our part, repudiate the criminal act. If this aggressive repudiation is necessary, it amounts to a confession that otherwise we should be liable to do the act ourselves. What other need can there be for punitive repudiation, for this violent denial of condonement, unless it be that our position is insecure—that our own temptation to do likewise is a menace to our ego-control?

If this is indeed true, would it not be more appropriate to punish our own criminal id, to punish ourselves, instead of seeking this way out at the expense of a scapegoat?

Do we not thereby actually express upon him our own hate impulses—to teach him that hate impulses must on no account be expressed; and to ensure that we ourselves will not express them!

The attempt to justify retribution as reasonable is manifestly absurd. That the retributive element exists in the psychology of punishment there is no denying. It is an emotional force. I would criticize merely the attempt to rationalize it, to justify it, and to disguise it as a function of the reason.

In tracing the evolution of modern punishment, Prof. Hamon, of Brussels, starts with what he calls the reflex instinct of defence. To this succeeds vengeance, or the reaction at a longer interval. This, he says, is the basis of the most primitive of laws, the *lex talionis*.[2] Finally the law of retaliation (retribution) is developed and codified.

To pass on to the theory of:

Deterrence

Regarding the alleged deterrent effect upon those not yet caught or sentenced, it is recorded that in the good old days when men and boys were hanged in public for trifling offences against

[1] Clarke Hall Lecture of 1934, London.
[2] A. Hamon, *La Responsabilité* (November 1897).

property, it was well known that all the pickpockets in London would be upon the scene plying their trade upon the crowds that came to witness the execution of their less fortunate brethren. We have it on record that of 167 thieves prepared for hanging 164 had witnessed public executions for theft.

The commission of crimes, particularly of serious crimes, is due to inner, often unconscious, causes, and is not based upon anything so conscious or reasonable as a proper assessment of the probable consequences however horrible these may be. For a cause, whether a group cause or an individual criminal cause —be it only revenge—men will always be ready to risk death— witness the martyrs. If it were otherwise, if a nation really did succeed in training its individuals to behave in accordance with the dictates of reason and in obedience to the possible consequences to themselves of their action, such a nation would find none of its enlightened law-fearing members prepared to go to war on its behalf. No doubt this would be equally a consequence of successfully learning the lesson of deterrence.

With all their hopes of deterrence by legal punishment, the nations still have *incurables* ready to be disembowelled on the barbed wire of no-man's-land.

Reformation

This theory must be based upon the hope that the aggressive or sadistic act has, after all, not been damaging; that it has, on the contrary, really benefited and improved the victim. Reality evidence apparently has little effect upon a belief which promises so much emotional advantage necessary to the placation of the superego or ego. Therefore, there is the tendency to cling to this satisfaction in spite of all the evidence to the contrary.

We should expect to find the reformatory principle most successful in the punishment of youthful offenders, but when Henry Mayhew visited a school under the Reformatory School Act of 1854, he wrote of it as follows: ' True the place is called a "House of Correction", but rightly viewed it is simply a criminal preparatory school where students are qualified for matriculating at Millbank or Pentonville.' This is due to the punishment compulsion entering into and vitiating the best reformatory intentions.

Punishment, the outward equivalent of total repression,

precludes sublimation or reform. If not a physical injury or castration (vide II), it appears to be a mental equivalent of this. I have clinical evidence that such measures, rigorously enforced from earliest infancy with the best intentions, have been directly responsible for a stunting of psychological growth in their victim.

The case I refer to is that of a woman who in consequence of a strict prison-like upbringing has been left with no originality or initiative. Her tendency is to find some mother or governess surrogate to issue orders for her to obey. The impression is that so far as her individuality and happiness are concerned she would have been better served by total destruction.

As previously quoted from Bernard Shaw: 'To punish is to injure; to reform is to heal. You cannot mend a person by damaging him.'

4. THE PSYCHOLOGY OF THE PUNISHED

An interesting confirmation of the ego-less origin of the psychology of legal punishment is that it fails to take into consideration the nature of the human material with which it deals. The ignoring of such a relevant reality factor is characteristic of the unconscious. 'Justice', like the unconscious, is depicted as being blind to reality.

The psychology of the punished has had much attention, and this paper is primarily on the psychology of the punisher. Therefore, the subject of this section will be dealt with only very briefly.

It is recognized by analysts that the position an individual gets himself into, his role in life, the things he does and often the things that happen to him, are on the whole mostly engineered by himself, consciously or unconsciously. It does not necessarily follow that the person who gets himself punished is invariably a masochist seeking this particular role and this particular mode of gratification. It is normal to seek advantages for oneself and to avoid disadvantages. Delinquents are, for the most part, seeking personal advantages.

They will, like these others, be motivated by their emotional needs and by their reality needs. There will be unconscious factors and ego factors responsible for their activity and for their getting themselves into the position of the punished.

The person whose unconscious urge for advantage is strong and whose ego is alive to reality will be unlikely to get himself into a position which is the exact opposite to that towards which his whole psyche is striving. The person who gets punished will, therefore, either be one whose emotional needs are abnormal (masochistic) or one whose ego is defective—or both—one who has not succeeded in coping with reality in accordance with his emotional requirements.

A sadist, for instance, who gets himself into a position appropriate for a masochist has failed in the ego-function of adjusting reality to his needs. Such failures imply ego-defect. It therefore does not surprise us to learn from Dr Penrose's statistical paper that in those countries where the asylums are relatively empty, the prisons are relatively full and vice versa.[1]

Nevertheless, I feel that the tendency would be to overestimate the importance of the ego as a responsible factor in punishment. There is much evidence that it is, particularly in the case of those who get punished, merely a tool in the hands of powerful unconscious desires and compulsions. As the goal achieved is that of being punished we expect to find that these persons, ego-defect or not, are, for the most part, masochistic.

The late Dr Morton, who had a lifelong experience as prison doctor and warden, revealed very clearly that a large number of prisoners were self-mutilators. One of many cases that he instanced was that of S.F., who swallowed a wire and had to be operated on for obstruction. Subsequently the man swallowed a spoon. At another laparotomy four spoons and an open safety-pin were removed. Again later when awaiting trial at the Quarter Sessions and while on hunger strike he swallowed four large nails. Eventually he developed a faecal fistula in the anterior abdominal wall. This man had been convicted again and again, and every medical officer found that he was neither insane nor a mental defective; perhaps they recognized that his psychological make-up was common to many delinquents.

It is interesting to hear that many of the self-mutilators concentrated attention upon their genital organs. Cases were recorded of wire being pushed into the bladder and numerous cases of opening the scrotum with scissors and of removal of the

[1] *Brit. J. Med. Psychol.*, 18, 1.

testes. It only needs to be added that these persons were only doing to themselves, and also getting the surgeons to do to them, the very mutilations which in the old days they got the law as a willing accomplice to do to them. And may it not be that in engineering, consciously or unconsciously, a crime, a trial and a punishment, they are still today seducing the community into inflicting equivalent damage or mental mutilations upon them?[1]

Apart from the fact that some persons (on account of unconscious guilt, etc.) actively *want* punishment and *must* see that they get it, there exists a large class of persons who are normally desirous of death. Only occasionally does this desire find expression in the form of suicide. It is noteworthy that one in every ninety deaths in Great Britain is due to suicide—a larger proportion than is popularly supposed. There is also the far larger class who do not actually commit suicide, but who put themselves in the way of death, and eventually achieve it by 'accident'. Then there is the still larger class whose behaviour shows a compromise between this death-desire and tendencies to self-preservation. Such persons get themselves into ill-health, tuberculosis, alcoholism, drug addiction, bankruptcy, misery or imprisonment. Now members of this large class of persons are not likely to be deterred by the prospect of misfortune, legally inflicted punishment or hanging. On the contrary, they are more likely to be unconsciously attracted by these possibilities or likelihoods. In these cases punishment, far from being a deterrent, is likely to be an incentive to their crime.

It is interesting to note here that where the punishment has exceeded the unconscious requirements of the delinquent, most notably in the cases where corporal punishment has been administered, the practical effect is often similar to the effect of crime upon the righteous—a fierce resolution for revenge.

I am told by prison visitors that the man who has received the 'cat' can often be detected by the expression on his face, and is ever after regarded by the warders as a dangerous prisoner liable to attack them or anybody if opportunity permits. They agree that even the birch makes any sort of treatment thereafter quite impossible.

[1] Cf. Freud, *Some Character Types met with in Psycho-Analytical Work.*

The punisher has failed to take this very evident psychology into consideration in his (compulsive) advocacy of punishment and in his rationalisation of his need to inflict it under the plea that it is wholly justified by deterrent effects. Is his blindness to the psychology of those he punishes due to emotional pleasure-principle requirements within himself? To requote Melanie Klein: 'Children who, unconsciously, were expecting to be cut to pieces, beheaded, devoured and so on, would feel compelled to be naughty and to get punished.'

But in whatever way the prisoner unconsciously engineers his punishment or unconsciously asks society to punish him, this does not justify a would-be sane society in yielding to his request. In our therapeutic or reformatory treatment of patients we do not demonstrate love to those who ask for it, or hate to those who demand it. A psycho-therapist who acted in this fashion would indeed himself have entered the emotional dog-fight and we should rightly judge him to be as much in need of psychotherapeutic treatment as the patient he was treating.

That such is actually the psychological position of a society that punishes is borne out by its failure to cure, reform, or even to understand its criminals.

5. CLINICAL EVIDENCE OF THE PSYCHOLOGY OF PUNISHMENT

Having briefly reviewed samples of the relevant objective data and having disposed of the rationalizations of the old penology, we will now turn to an example of the clinical material that throws so much light on the psychology of punishment.

The patient, a pale, intense young man, exhibits an extraordinary amount of anxiety at his first interview. It appears that his nervousness is due to the constant anticipation of punishment by me.

On his way to see me he recollected an incident when he secretly put on the trousers of a young man he admired and caned himself through them with erotic results. This happened five years ago, but the thought of having to confess it to me nearly caused him to turn back.

'What did you think I would do?'

'I thought you would jump up and throw me out,'

His stammer and tremor and obsession with sexual guilt indicate that unconsciously he expects castration.

He says that his acquaintances, etc. (he can hardly be said to have friends), think him too good to live—he never so much as looks at a woman; but he knows himself to be a 'terrible homosexual'. It appears that he would be better described as an asexual or anti-sexual, for he has never participated in any sort of sexual act with another person. He proved to be a repressed sadist.

It appears that he has successfully repressed or inhibited every tendency to heterosexuality and even to homosexuality, and is using the remainder of his mental energy to combat his component instincts.

His reason for seeking advice is a fear that in some form or another these impulses may attain some sort of expression. His method is to avoid any stimulating experience. In consequence taboos have been accumulating. For instance, he dare not attend cricket matches, which he used to enjoy, because of the sight of a young man in flannel trousers bending down. He dare not pass through streets with shop windows because of the possibility of there being a cane or stick on exhibition. But the worst phobia of all, and one it is not always possible to avoid, is the dreadful apparition of a man with a whip riding behind a horse. This has occasioned many a hurried excursion down a side street.

The fantasy in this connection is as follows: the man might at any time strike the horse with his whip. In that event the patient felt he would be unable to resist the impulse to fly at that man and *lash him to death*. 'To kill the man who beat the horse' became at one time a nuclear phrase in his analysis.

And then an interesting fact emerged. It appears that this patient had, in childhood, beaten a horse until he had exhausted himself and lamed the animal.

The psychology of this phobia is self-evident. His sadistic desire, in spite of the displacements which it had previously undergone, has been repressed and anti-cathected. His superego now takes up the beating—and has, incidentally, 'beaten', not only his ego, but even the source of his instinctive life into a condition of perhaps permanent injury. This superego is, nevertheless, for ever on the watch lest this crime, to which his id is so prone, should again occur. Also it may be that the beating-instinct itself, in spite of its superego disguise, is also for ever on the watch to achieve its relief. The opportunity comes when the *crime* is discovered being perpetrated by *another* .Through the mechanisms of projection the id, or the id-tolerant ego, can now be attacked in the form of a scapegoat. The instinct tension in its superego disguise can now achieve its outlet, and the much needed relief to the psyche can be gained at the expense of this 'other' criminal.

The only practical difficulty in the way of this health-giving process is the ego or the reality principle. To lash to death men who strike a horse in the street is not sensible or practical. But what if some device can be invented whereby it might seem sensible and be made practical!

Where the desire is strong and the need for relief imperative, all the resources of the ego will be endlessly pressed into its service. 'Where there's a will there's a way.' Organized communities have found such a way in the paraphernalia of legal punishment. Our patient, being individual and less powerful, had resource only to fantasy. However much his positive Oedipus wishes urged him to destroy the man with the whip (in the last analysis obviously a father-with-phallus symbol), the pleasure-seeking element in his Oedipus complex had undergone too much repression, too much whipping, to seek any person in the image of his mother.

Furthermore, aided by the formal canings received during childhood from his father (who, incidentally, was a jurist), this patient had acquired some of the psychology of him-who-must-be-punished. He had inverted his Oedipus complex and received much pleasure from fantasies which followed the lines of those early experiences at the hands of his father. Nevertheless, there was still the tendency to play the active role, the role of his father, and himself administer the beating. He can do this if he substitutes his own buttocks for the passive role of the mother. He has done all this in the incident which he first confessed.

At the same time, in the same act, he combined his sadistic impulse with retributive punishment for it. To beat oneself is *to beat* and, at the same time, *to be beaten for it*.

Of course, at a deeper level it is the complete sexual act of the infant with himself in the dual role of father and mother.

In spite of all its advantages, this is not entirely satisfactory or ego-syntonic. The process again tends to be projected outwards so far as fear and opportunity will permit. His pleasure-giving fantasy is neither that of beating a horse nor that of beating the horse-beater. The former, like heterosexuality, is forbidden, and there is little libidinal satisfaction in the latter. It is just a compulsion that has to be obeyed. The favourite pleasure-giving fantasy is that of beating the buttocks of an attractive young man, a man resembling his past self or what he would like to have been. The only way in which this is permitted to take place, even in fantasy, is rather complicated. It is worth studying, as it reveals more of the mental mechanisms at work in the individual patient and in the community.

First of all it is essential that the young man should have performed a criminal act, for, to beat or punish an innocent person would be to place oneself in the wrong, and that would be to reverse the whole process.[1]

Compare here the elaborate legal and popular emphasis placed on the distinction of guilt and innocence; nothing is too bad for the guilty, nothing too good for the innocent. Psychoanalysis teaches us to distrust these valuations.

The crime allotted to the young man is, of course, that of having beaten the horse as the patient did when he was young. (In the last analysis: sadistic incest-guilt.) The most stringent safeguards must be taken against guilt in himself. The responsibility for the punishment is transferred to a magistrate or judge. It is essential that the cloak of legal justice should cover the libidinal nature of the act about to take place. (Deeper analysis is here not essential for the purpose of revealing the psychology of punishment.) Finally, in an atmosphere of high moral indignation, the judge orders our patient to perform the punishment.

Even then there are further safeguards. There is a tendency, in the patient as in the jurist, to justify the procedure in the eyes of the world and particularly in the eyes of the victim (though

---

[1] This can be done and enjoyed, but it is contrary to the trend of the above fantasy. This reversibility of punishment is noteworthy outside the consulting room. One may recall the case of Horatio Bottomley who, as editor of *John Bull* and as public speaker, was loudest in his condemnation of 'scandalous swindlers'. Subsequently he was convicted of the very type of crime which he had most hotly condemned. Perhaps, similarly, we often find those who advocate the rod commonly boasting of having received it in childhood.

really in the eyes of his own superego.) Compare here the theories produced to justify legal punishment (vide III). Speeches are made to the effect that it is a necessary matter, that it is for the victim's good, etc.—much as his father made before the canings of his childhood. These earned merely the child's contempt. He intuitively recognized them as manifestations of his father's guilt-anxiety.

There is a long period of conflict in the patient's mind, dramatized in the form of these safeguards, and a long period of pleasure in the form of preparation. (Compare here the legal procedure of safeguards—lengthy trials and delayed executions.)

Finally, the superego, having been placated or reassured that the beating is in accordance with the highest superego principles —that there are no id desires responsible for it—then, and then only, may the act take place.

Needless to say, it is, even in fantasy, accompanied by erotic excitement and orgasm. (Compare here the public excitement which accompanied the ancient legal barbarities—vide II. A further degree of repression produces the neurosis from which the modern prison staff is said to suffer at the time of a flogging or execution.)

To summarize briefly the psychopathology of this case, we may divide it into three stages.

In the first stage we perceive the infant with his aggressive instinct becoming prematurely libidinized, or his sexual impulse carrying with it a great deal of infantile aggression.

Libidinal development is largely fixated at an anal-sadistic stage, while a portion of it approaches phallic expression; he arrives at a desire to do something to his mother's anus, symbolized by her buttocks. On account of repression this part-object becomes displaced and identified with an animal—the horse. When he comes for treatment it is still the horse's buttocks which are of special interest. In this guise he presently gave expression to the original impulse when he indulged in the orgy of horse-beating. Later the identification with his own buttocks reveals itself.

The second stage, interlacing with the first, is the stage of repression. Strong measures are required to cope with the sadistic impulses that would destroy his mother, overwhelm his ego and destroy himself. The aggressive elements of his sadistic impulses are transferred to his superego to keep in check these same sadistic impulses.

We have noticed the earliest influence of this process in occasioning a prohibition of the fantasies directed to his mother and, consequently, a displacement on to the horse. Repression did its work so well that all females, being in the shape of mother, were prohibited even in fantasy.

There is abundant evidence of this stage throughout the long period of his childhood and adolescence. For instance: he spends his school holidays in an agony of trying to avoid the sight of two moles on his mother's neck. The thought had come to him that here he was suckled (he already dare not know where her breasts are), and if he looks, dreadful things will happen to him.

We discovered, moreover, that caning is still going on in his unconscious. Lying on the analytical settee he finds that he is not relaxing but is instead holding his buttocks in a state of tense rigidity. It transpires that he comes to his sessions as though he were coming to be caned and lies there with rigid muscles as though I were actually caning him. 'Prison-life' is already being experienced and further punishment anticipated.

The third stage is one of attempted release for (a) repressed aggression and (b) repressed libido.

Aggressive Instincts

If he can go back to the Oedipus situation and undo his own castration anxieties, if, instead of murdering his own sexuality, he can go back and vent his aggression in castrating the father (the man who beats the horse), that alone will be some relief.

In the third stage he discovers that somebody else, some id, is performing those very acts which he wants to do but must not do. His aggression, denied his id and transferred to his superego, has at last discovered a means of directing itself outwards instead of inwards. By utilizing the scapegoat his psyche can obtain a much-needed satisfaction and relief.

Bottled-up aggression, like bottled-up sexuality, tends to be orgastic in its discharge; hence no punishment can be too bad for the culprit; hence the savage mutilations of the past embodied in the legal code of those times. Hence the intolerance of the punisher at any attempt to deprive him of his fullest expression. Though we may be constrained to temper 'justice' by substituting for it an alternative emotional gratification—mercy—we are not prepared to forego these pleasures altogether by substituting reason.

Sexual Instincts

In a psyche trodden down by a severe superego or in an individual trodden down by a severe law, the aggressive instinct is not the only one straining at the bars of its prison. The libidinal or pleasure-seeking instincts are also seeking some measure of gratification that may elude superego vigilance. This can best be done if they too can persuade the superego that they are acting on its own behalf. This is a more difficult task, but there are several mechanisms at work which render it not too difficult. The first to be pressed into service is the mechanism of projection.

Already the superego has learned to liberate id-aggression provided it is the hated id-aggression *in another* that is being attacked. Supposing the person displaying this id-aggression is not the hated father, but is the love-object, the mother, the person whom there would be so much sadistic enjoyment in attacking. Are we going to waive this rare opportunity of gratifying an impulse so highly charged, so intolerably repressed, now that the superego has given its permission to attack?

As one would expect, the opportunity is seized with alacrity, but various precautions are instituted to put the superego off the scent of libidinous id-impulses. The object about to be attacked or punished, in so far as it is a love-object, is treated to a process to convince the punisher's superego that no ulterior motive is at work. The word 'justice' is much stressed (by the mind of patient and jurist). The whole process is so encumbered or manacled by rules and precautions (the products of the opposition) that it can move only very slowly towards its goal. This is invariably the goal of the instinct that initiated the movement.

This is obvious in the case of our patient, for however deferred, the goal is inevitably orgasm. But, unless we stress terminology too much, perversions need not necessarily be complete substitutes for the sexual act. Pleasure-seeking can attain a considerable degree of substitute satisfaction. This may be regarded as forepleasure or tumescence, leaving at least detumescence to the sexual act proper.[1]

There is, however, one conspicuous difference between the psychology of this patient and that of punishment and legal procedure. In spite of all his superego deceptions he does not *entirely* delude his ego. He knows that his fantasy is really pleasure-seeking.

In the legal rationalization of punishment we are attempting to endow an instinctive emotional reaction with all the majesty of a reasoned and logical process.

As in the case of my patient, the sword of the id has been taken over by the superego, and the primitive aggression, with its variable degree of libidinal accompaniment, will now be used in the name of Justice or God.

6. DISCUSSION AND RECAPITULATION

As the id is the psychological[2] source of all impulse — of all behaviour — a review of the psychology of punishment should begin with its source in the id. (Later its progress and modifications through other levels of the mental apparatus may be traced.)

THE ID

Aggressive Instincts

Reviewing the material provided — historical and clinical — it appears that the aggressive or destructive instinct is principally responsible for the phenomenon of punishment as it is at the root, also, of much criminal behaviour.

We know this about the aggressive or destructive instinct, that whether it has a primary nucleus or not (whether or not there is such a thing as the death-instinct) there can be no doubt that aggression is at least enormously stimulated, exacerbated, or perhaps even called into being by any and every instinct—frustration.

---

[1] It was jestingly said of one of our deceased judges that whenever he pronounced the death sentence he simultaneously experienced ejaculation.

[2] It would be an added interest to trace these forces from their pre-psychological, their somatic, sources. Certainly it is evident that various somatic differences, such as differences in glandular balance, can make differences in the quality and quantity of these forces. Thus one might conclude that it would be as illogical to punish an organ for disease as an organism (an individual) for delinquency.

What frustration was, or is, society suffering from that its aggressive instinct *demands* an excuse for expression—be it law or war?

We may note at once that the avowed object of law is frustration, deterrence. Hence we see that society living under its own laws is enduring from this source a frustration, which in its young days at least it could bear only with difficulty, and then only provided some outlet was periodically permitted for those very instincts which the law frustrated.

The id, labouring under the frustration of its aggressive instincts by the law, was pressing for a release or outlet for those instincts whose quality and tension had been so heightened by law-frustration. In so far as it did not itself infringe the law it found an outlet for this aggression in two sociological directions; one was war, and the other was, ingeniously, an aggressive infliction of the law in the form of punishment. Judges and jurists are still jealous of this privileged mode of tension-relief for themselves and will defend it with every possible rationalization. If we cannot bear to suffer the endopsychic tension consequent upon the frustration of our aggressive or destructive instinct, then indeed somebody or something must suffer and be injured, be it the accused or be it some other nation. It is certainly safer to destroy accused *individuals*. The subtlety of this mental manoeuvre of venting our law-repressed aggression upon him who has infringed the law is certainly not all the function of the id alone. The id is concerned merely with pressing the ego towards the relief of instinct tension. The mechanisms which lead to that mode of relief assuming the form of legal punishment is a matter to be discussed under superego and ego. But I would say here that the id does achieve such relief whenever injury or destructive behaviour, such as punishment, is expressed, and it makes no difference to the satisfaction of the id whether the expression be anti-legal or legal, whether it be criminal act, punishment or war.

The subtlety of legal punishment lies in the fact that while it is law which, by enforcing suppression of instinct relief, thereby stimulates and increases the aggressive instinct, it is also law which, by enjoining punishment, permits an outlet for this aggression in its augmented violence.

We are beginning to see an analogy between the phenomenon

of legal punishment and a symptom, for even at this stage it has the characteristic of expressing the instinct to which it has forbidden expression, of achieving the forbidden gratification.

Sexual Instincts

The other powerful instinct that has its source within the id is the libidinal, sexual, or pleasure-seeking instinct. Does punishment derive any of its drive from this source? Does the infliction of punishment bring any relief or gratification to this instinct?

There can be no doubt about the answer in the case of my patient with the horse-beating complex. His chief mode of sexual gratification is beating or punishing fantasies. He has only so much as to think of striking a bottom with a cane, and he immediately experiences erection. By means of the fantasy complete orgasm is obtained.

It seems probable that his father, a jurist, was not entirely free from, at least unconscious, libidinal relief, when he periodically subjected his sons to a caning ritual. It seems probable that the public, who only a few centuries ago tied naked people to carts and beat them, found some libidinal pleasure in the process. Spectators who paid two shillings for seats round Tyburn Tree were evidently prompted by their pleasure-seeking instincts. Our modern jurists in ordering punishment, conspicuously such punishment as the 'cat', and those who inflict it or witness it, are probably not immune to, at least, a *conflict* in which the libidinal instinct, as well as the aggressive, plays a considerable part. My clinical experience has opened my eyes to the fact that conflict even to the degree of conscious agony does not preclude the possibility of considerable unconscious libidinal relief actually accompanying it. For instance, I have a female patient suffering from total psycho-sexual frigidity who spends her analytical session literally writhing in an agony of frustration and yet becomes angry and violent if it is so much as suggested to her that she should forego a session. Analysis reveals that under the conscious agony of resistance there exists simultaneously a gratifying though repressed fantasy containing all the joys of sexual indulgence. At a very deep level she is experiencing her early incestuous intercourse, while at the same time at a slightly less deep level is the resistance due to the fantasy of the terrifying eyes of her mother. The agony of this situation fills consciousness, whilst the id-gratification of the act remains repressed, but none the less gratifying. Moreover, this is the only way in which she can reduce her instinct-tension; and so we can better understand the violence of her insistence upon it. Hence the pain which the punisher feels or claims to feel ('It hurts me as much as it hurts you') does not preclude the presence of deep libidinal satisfaction.

Newspapers that specialize in catering for the emotional needs of the public do not hesitate to give priority to the most lurid crime. Crime and *punishment* are usually the richest emotional diet unless the international news promises something of a similarly stimulating nature.

The Superego

The function of this level of the mind in the psychology of punishment has been sufficiently stressed throughout this paper. Punishment is, of course, the special proclivity of the superego. The superego comes into being at the instigation of the parents or parent surrogates, by the energy of the id going over to the other side (anti-cathexis) and being directed against the id.

Instead of fighting for our (original) selves against the parents (or state) we are now fighting for the parents (or state) against our (original) selves. It is still 'fighting' that is going on, and it is still the same weapons that are being used. It is still the same satisfactions that are being achieved—especially if we can find an external representative of our original selves to attack. Thus, at the expense of the scapegoat, or criminal, we are still satisfying our primitive instincts, now cloaked as superego activities, and calling the process 'punishment' instead of 'crime'.

THE EGO

Punishment is so fully explained on the basis of id and superego activity that it seemed to me difficult to see what the ego or reason had to do with it. Yet the ego must come into the picture if only on account of the fact that it has given sanction to the unconscious urges. Then it occurred to me that if we ask anybody who is not primarily a psychologist for an explanation of the phenomenon of punishment, he will reply, or endeavour to reply, in terms of its ego-psychology.

It would be easy to find many such replies that were as symptomatic or even psychotic as the most sadistic punishment of bygone ages, but these would be merely of subjective interest. Looking for a reply that might contain something at least of objective or real value, I thought of the first Clarke Hall Lecture on the Ethics of Penal Action delivered by the then Archbishop of York in 1934.

You will remember that the late Clarke Hall was the magistrate above all others who tried to introduce modern psychological enlightenment into his treatment of delinquents, and the Clarke Hall Fellowship was founded to further his life's endeavours.

Now the attitude of the intelligent non-psychologist to which the then Archbishop of York in this lecture showed himself to be no exception, is briefly this: What I (think and) do is reasonable and right, and what the State does is, in the main, reasonable and right. The State exacts certain punishments, therefore it must be reasonable and right to punish in the way the State does punish. We shall proceed to justify the State.

As one might expect the result is a collection of clever *rationalizations*. It occurs to me that had the learned Archbishop lived and lectured a hundred odd years ago he would have found no difficulty in rationalizing, in explaining and justifying, in terms of ego-psychology and reason, the obviously sadistic barbarities of that age. In 1826 an Archbishop and six Bishops lent their support to Lord Ellenborough when he insisted that to repeal capital punishment for petty theft would deliver every shopkeeper into the hands of the unscrupulous. Hanging for petty theft was justified as an act of the ego or reason.

To take one most plausible illustration from the Archbishop of York's lecture: 'If we are to think clearly at all on this subject, we must begin with a sharp distinction between revenge and punishment. Suppose that two boys at school are quarrelling. One insults the other; the other retaliates with a blow. He may say that he was punishing a fellow for insulting him; but, in fact, he is exacting vengeance. Now suppose that they start fighting in earnest, and that the Headmaster comes upon them, stops the fight and punishes them for fighting when the rules or discipline of the school forbid this. His action is a true infliction of punishment. *He has no injury of his own to avenge* . . . There is here no revenge either wild or civilized. The difference is fundamental.'

I am not concerned with the schoolmaster but only with the logic of the argument. 'He punishes them for fighting when the rules or discipline of the school forbid this. He has no injury of his own to avenge.'

But has he no injury of his own to avenge? Did not he establish the rules or discipline of the school which the culprits are destroying? Is it not essential to the maintenance of *his* power and of *his* peace of mind that these rules and discipline should be preserved? In fighting each other they are, therefore, assailing his rule, assailing his power, the principle for which he stands. Each boy was trying to convince the other that it was injurious to assail his power. The Headmaster is trying to convince them both that it is injurious to assail *his* power. There is no difference in principle. May we suspect the Archbishop of a very natural bias in favour of the Headmaster?

But apart from all this there can be something much deeper in the infliction of even apparently disinterested punishment, whether by subordinates or by the State. When my patient has an impulse to kill the man who beat the horse, is he also a disinterested dispenser of justice? He is apparently neither the beater nor the horse, just as the schoolmaster is neither the victim nor the delinquent. But this is only an appearance based on conscious psychology. From our analysis of the patient we *know* that, psychologically speaking, he is *both the beater and the horse*. We are not then surprised to find that he is incapable of feeling or acting rationally and is certainly not qualified for the god-like role of a disinterested dispenser of justice. Like the State or the schoolmaster he is driven by the forces of an unconscious conflict between his id and his superego.

The fact is that, consciously or unconsciously, these identifications are bound to take place, and the practical truth is that, whether we know it or not, they vitiate our ability to react dispassionately to another's aggression or delinquency. Pure reason does not in practice command the situation. Like the delinquent, our reason is driven by unconscious forces—mostly conflicting forces.

It is clear that the majority of human beings, however intelligent, are victims of a mass suggestion, with the result that they unconsciously identify themselves with the State, and establish the institutions and customs of the State as the criterion of what is right and good. As psychologists we fail if we fall into this trap, and I think few of us escape scot-free. The force of it is too great.

Perhaps we, too, a few hundred years ago would have extolled, or at least condoned, justified or rationalized, such things as the sadistic examination and burning of witches.

We are still faced with the question: What activity *can* we assess to the ego (or reason) in this phenomenon of punishment? Let us see what the id or superego *would* do to the delinquent if left to itself, if no ego existed, and then let us see what we actually do to him. The difference will represent ego activity in some form.

It is id-aggression handed over to the super-ego which finds its outlet, the relief of endo-psychic tension, in the infliction of punishment upon the *manifest* id, which latter is identified with the criminal through his criminal act. What an opportunity to indulge with full superego sanction in this destructive hate impulse which we have unconsciously bottled up only too long! And in the good old days we eagerly seized upon this opportunity and freely and openly indulged in this destruction, as has been described in the history of the punishments of those days. The position at the present time is that, unfortunately for us, we cannot give such free rein to this lust, and still maintain the self-deception that we are not criminal, but anti-criminal dispensers of a god-like justice.

To obtain an outlet for our criminality and sadism we now require a better disguise, before they can pass the more alert censorship of the ego, before they can overcome ego-resistance. Therefore we have installed a more refined *mental* torture in their place.

The function of the ego in the phenomenon of punishment is therefore seen to be in the nature of a resistance to a too conspicuous revelation of id-aggression, sometimes even in its super-ego displacement. Superego devices no longer seem completely to disguise it, if it savours too strongly of sadistic id-equivalents. The id-aggression, whether in its original form or whether on the side of the angels (superego), would undoubtedly seize the

F   81

opportunity to rend its victim (the criminal) to pieces, to disembowel him, to castrate him, to devour him, as the Roman wild animals—acting as proxies for the spectators—devoured the victims thrown to them.

Bernard Shaw says that if you punish a man retributively, you must injure him. If you are to reform him, you must improve him. And men are not improved by injuries.

It is chiefly the ego which says 'No. This would be too apparent, too suspect. If we must destroy him, let it be his mind rather than his body, then no blood will be spilt, and our aggressive instinct will escape detection.'

How unpopular will be the spoil-sport person who declares: 'Why, you have given the game away by the very use of that word "Punishment". Punishment *means* destruction. The sufferer knows it intuitively, why delude yourselves?'

Let us recognize the two essential truths that emerge from an analytical examination of the problem of crime and punishment. One is that the delinquent in his action against us is driven by unconscious forces. And the second is that we in our action against him are no less driven by similar unconscious forces.

A recognition of these two complementary truths is essential for a consideration of ego-function in dealing with delinquency and crime, and for a possibility of its practical application.

III

The Fundamental Nature of Anxiety

With regard to the relationship of anxiety to the production of psychogenic symptoms, Freud (1936, p. 119) has said: 'There seem to be two very widely held opinions . . . one is that anxiety is itself a neurotic symptom. The other is that . . . symptoms are only formed in order to avoid anxiety; they bind the mental energy which would otherwise be discharged as anxiety. Thus anxiety *would be the fundamental phenomenon and main problem of neurosis.*' (My italics.)

He goes on to say that there are grounds for the second opinion in that if a phobic patient is made to face his phobic situation, or if an obsessional neurotic is prevented from washing his hands, each will become a prey to almost unbearable anxiety. In other words, symptomatology, of these types of illness at least, is built up merely as a protection against the fundamental anxiety.

If anxiety is the fundamental phenomenon underlying all nervous and mental disturbances, if it is 'the main problem of neurosis', the fundamental nature of anxiety itself clearly has priority in its demand for investigation.

Confusion has arisen in the literature regarding this question of the fundamental nature of anxiety through writers introducing innumerable *consequences* and elaborate *constructions arising from,* or accompanying, anxiety as though they revealed its fundamental nature. As it appears that everything nervous and mental can arise in consequence of anxiety, there is obviously no limit to which this confusion can progress. Under the title of anxiety, or aspects of anxiety, we might indeed rewrite almost the entire literature of neuroses, psychoneuroses and psychoses.

It is clear that there are at least two opposite ways in which we can discuss the phenomenon of anxiety. The first may be called the 'constructive method', namely, constructively building upon it all the elaborate phenomena of clinical psychology. This seems to be what most psychological writers use, sometimes without recognizing that they are not necessarily elucidating the nature of anxiety itself. The second method of investigating anxiety I would call the 'reductive method', meaning an attempt to get down to its primary nature. I do not think that this has been sufficiently seriously attempted. It may be because along this pathway we are soon stopped at the frontiers of chemistry and physics. Nevertheless, until we can go further in this direction, the elaborate edifice of our clinical psychology is built upon a very airy and perhaps impractical foundation. I think we might at least examine this foundation, even if we have to call in physiology and the natural sciences to complete the examination.

BRIEF REVIEW

Before we start, let us briefly review what contributions have been offered by psychologists in the attempt to solve the problem of the basic nature of anxiety.

Hinsie's (1940) *Psychiatric Dictionary* gives the origin of 'anxiety' as from the Latin *anxietas,* meaning distressed state. *Anxus* is the past participle of *angere*, meaning to throttle, choke, cause pain. I think this derivation is of biological interest. It suggests a relationship between literal, physical choking and the suppression or frustration of emotional outlets. Either of these would obviously cause increased tension, acute discomfort, or overt anxiety—perhaps amounting to a sense of impending death. Hinsie goes on to define 'anxiety': 'Mental energy belonging to the instincts may be transformed into affects. Anxiety is one of the affects.' He then attempts a more elaborate definition: 'In the process of repression the ideational presentation of an instinct vanishes from consciousness (if it were ever there) . . . Three courses are then open for the instinctual part of the ideational presentation. It may be suppressed entirely; it may appear "in the guise of an affect of a particular qualitative tone"; it may be transformed into anxiety.'

McDougall (1926) defines anxiety as 'An emotional state that is apt to arise whenever some strong continuing desire appears likely to fail to attain its goal.'

Rank (1929) naturally relates it to the birth trauma, and to the subsequent loss of the former security and freedom from effort and disturbance that was present in the womb and that has now given place to feelings of helplessness.

Bleuler (1930) thinks it has different sources, and says that in some cases it is connected with respiratory difficulties, but goes on to say that it is undoubtedly connected in some way with sexuality.

Fenichel (1946, p. 132) says: 'The problem of anxiety is the essence of any psychology of neurotic conflict. The primary anxiety or the first experiences out of which later anxiety develops is the manifestation of *unmastered tension* . . . it can be understood partly as the way in which the unmastered tension makes itself felt, and partly as an expression of vegetative emergency discharge.' He speaks also of 'tamed' anxiety developed by the ego in case of danger as an 'anxiety signal', a preparation for defence, and goes on to say that 'anxiety is a fear of experiencing a traumatic state, or the possibility that the organisation of the ego may be overwhelmed by excitation'. When writing of 'emotional spells' as involuntary discharges of anxiety tension (1946, p. 120), he suggests that 'the archaic epileptic syndrome probably functions as an emergency outlet in certain constitutionally predisposed individuals'.

As regards the fundamental nature of anxiety, Freud has produced considerable clarification and admitted some puzzlement. First of all he made the whole thing simple, up to a point, by saying that anxiety arose from a transformation of repressed libido; next he denied all that, said it was nothing of the sort, but that anxiety was purely a *reaction of the ego* to an external or internal situation and must be regarded as having its source in the ego. Anxiety was thus a *cause* of repression and not a result of it. Thirdly, he appears to have been at some pains to reconcile these two apparently contradictory statements, and finally assumed that each has a place.

For instance, in the *New Introductory Lectures* Freud (1933, p. 109) said: 'Children's phobias, and the anxiety expectation in anxiety neurosis serve as two examples of one way in which neurotic anxiety comes about; i.e. through direct transformation of libido.' Some years later in *Inhibitions, Symptoms and Anxiety* (1936, p. 54) he deliberately makes this opposite statement and follows it by a series of retractions throughout the book: 'Anxiety never arises from repressed libido. If I had formerly been content to say that after the occurrence of repression there appeared, in place of the manifestation of libido that was to be expected, a certain amount of anxiety, I should have nothing to retract today. The description would be correct; and there does undoubtedly exist a correspondence of the kind asserted between the strength of the impulse that has to be repressed and the intensity of the resultant anxiety. But I must admit that I thought I was giving more than a mere description. I believed I had put my finger on a metapsychological process of direct transformation of libido into anxiety. I can now no longer maintain this view. And, indeed, I found it impossible at the time to explain how a transformation of that kind was carried out.'

He goes on to say: 'I found that outbreaks of anxiety and a general state of anxiety-preparedness were produced . . . whenever sexual excitement was inhibited, arrested or deflected in its progress towards gratification. Since sexual excitement was an expression of libidinal instinctual impulses it did not seem too rash to assume that the libido was turned into anxiety through the agency of these disturbances. The observations which I made at the time still hold good. Moreover, it cannot be denied that the libido belonging to the id-processes is subjected to interruption at the instigation of repression. We can still maintain, therefore, that in repression anxiety is produced from the libidinal cathexes of the instinctual impulses. But how can we reconcile this conclusion with our other conclusion that the anxiety felt in phobias is an ego anxiety and arises in the ego, and that it does not proceed out of repression but, on the contrary, sets repression in motion? There seems to be a contradiction here which is not at all simple to solve. It will not be easy to reduce the two sources of anxiety to a single one. We might attempt to do so by supposing that, when coitus is disturbed or sexual excitement interrupted or abstinence enforced, the ego scents certain dangers to which it reacts with anxiety. But this takes us nowhere. On the other hand, our analysis of the phobias seems to admit of no correction. *Non liquet.*'

Having emphasized almost throughout the book that his latest view is that anxiety is a reaction of the ego and has its source in the ego and that anxiety never arises from repressed libido, Freud (1936, p. 114) goes on to say: 'It is still an undeniable fact that in sexual abstinence, improper interference with the processes of sexual excitation or deflexion of the latter from its psychological modification, *anxiety arises directly out of libido*; in other words, that the ego is reduced to a state of helplessness in the face of an excessive tension due to need, as it was in the situation of birth, and that anxiety is then produced. Here once more, though the matter is of little importance, it is very possible that *what finds discharge in anxiety is precisely the surplus of unutilised libido*. As we know, a psycho-neurosis is especially liable to develop on the basis of an actual neurosis. This looks as though the ego were attempting to save itself from anxiety, which it has learned to keep in suspension for a while, and to bind it by the formation of symptoms.' (My italics.)

Freud makes a clear distinction between reaction to external danger and reaction to internal danger; the former reaction is sometimes called objective anxiety, and the latter one neurotic anxiety. Later I hope to point out that *at a basic level* this distinction is unwarranted. At the same time I shall suggest that at this basic level the distinction between the two alleged sources of anxiety, libidinal and ego, is also unwarranted, and that Freud's honest puzzlement draws attention to a truth about the fundamental nature of anxiety; for at a basic level these distinctions do not exist. When there is any ground for them it is contingent upon developmental elaborations of psychic structure, and has to do with that structure and not with the fundamental nature of anxiety.

However, before leaving this matter of attempts of psychological writers to clarify anxiety we must mention the views of Melanie Klein (1948, p. 114). In 'A contribution to the theory of anxiety and guilt', after having referred to Freud's views, she comes to two conclusions: '(a) In young children it is unsatisfied libidinal excitation which turns into anxiety. (b) The earliest *content* of anxiety is the infant's feeling of danger lest his need should not be satisfied because the mother is "absent".'

[Regarding (a), 'unsatisfied libidinal excitation' obviously means a state of tension unrelieved. Perhaps the phenomena of anxiety may be regarded as the only outlet (or relief) for this tension. Regarding (b), the feeling of *danger* is clearly nothing more or less than an anticipation of (a).]

After obtaining considerable justification from Freud and

from Abraham, Melanie Klein (1932) put forward her hypothesis of what she considers to be the primary cause of anxiety, namely, 'Anxiety arises by the danger which threatens the organism from the *death instinct*'; and she repeats this view in a paper (1948, p. 116). She disagrees with Freud's statement that the fear of death should be regarded as analogous to the fear of castration, because she says, her analytical observations show that there is in the unconscious a fear of annihilation of life. She proceeds to say: 'Thus, in my view, the danger arising from the inner working of the death-instinct is the first cause of anxiety.'

She believes that anxiety arises from a conflict between life and death instincts, i.e. 'that in these anxieties aggression and the defences against it are of paramount importance'. 'The death instinct (destructive impulse) is the primary factor in the causation of anxiety.'

She says further (1948, p. 123): 'The primary object against which the destructive impulses are directed is the object of the libido . . . it is therefore the interaction between aggression and libido which causes anxiety and guilt.' And again: 'An optimum in the interaction between libido and aggression implied that the anxiety arising from the perpetual activity of the death instinct, though never eliminated, is counteracted and kept at bay by the power of the life instinct.'

We cannot go into Klein's interesting description of special forms of anxiety, such as persecutory anxiety, depressive anxiety and guilt, as these are examples of the familiar elaborations, leading us away from our study of the fundamental nature of anxiety.

So we see that even when trying to avoid the psychological superstructure of anxiety in case it should lead us away from fundamentals and into every nook and cranny of mental science, we nevertheless meet with considerable complexity—even where we had hoped for something simple and in keeping with biological knowledge, if not so fundamental as physiology and chemistry.

In spite of all that has been written, I have found myself, in the course of my clinical work, puzzling about anxiety, the most frequently met with of all clinical phenomena, just as though I had never heard of it before! If the basic nature of anxiety is clinically so unobvious, I would suggest that we have another look at objective reality to see if we can find any clue.

The fundamental nature of anxiety, like the nature of everything else, can best be understood by examining its evolutionary, phylogenetic or developmental origin.

A PHYLOGENETIC EXCURSION INTO BIOLOGY

Perhaps we cannot hope to find anything resembling anxiety in inanimate matter, though we do find something analogous to integration and conflict, namely, an interplay of forces, even of equal and opposite forces, such as the positive and negative charges within the atom. As soon as we get to the most complex chemico-physical substance, namely, protoplasm, we find certain chemically conditioned processes spontaneously at work involving interaction between it and its environment. Once some organization has taken place, even at virus level, we can see that the characteristic of the living process is a reaction upon its environment, directed towards building itself up at the expense of that environment. It assimilates matter and it grows. Of course, the process is chemically conditioned, but so for that matter is every living process, including that of mental functioning. I would suggest that the basic nature of the living process is essentially that of absorbing its environment, changing this into its own substance and *growing* at the expense of its environment.

So far there need be no mind, and, indeed, no nervous system or physical basis of mind. Yet even Protozoa, which have no organized nervous system, commonly run to some co-ordinating mechanism. In ciliates this takes the form of what is sometimes called a silver-line system. It is a system of proto-plasmic fibres which run longitudinally near the surface of the animal and connect rows of small granules at the bases of its cilia. Such a system has been termed a neuro-motor apparatus. Thereby the animal can move more quickly than the amoeba. The chief function which these primitive structural developments subserve is that of moving towards food and away from frustration, ultimately the function of growth. Vegetable life which has, of course, no nervous system, is similarly occupied in extracting from its environment material for its growth, but is relatively less capable of locomotion and of overcoming frustrations.

My contention is that when nervous structure and ultimately mind begin to develop, they serve the primary purpose of facilitating growth, and of overcoming frustrations that lie between the organism and this purpose. I cannot emphasize too strongly that under the term growth I would include reproduction, whether it is cell division in Protozoa, the branchings of a plant, shoot or slip (which, like all growth in metazoa, means no more or less than reproduction of its cellular components), or what we ordinarily know as reproduction in higher forms of life carried out by specialized organs.

Growth which I have regarded as the characteristic phenomenon of life includes a certain, as it were, *self-assertiveness* upon an object, however simply this self-assertiveness may be chemically conditioned. Every form of life is actively engaged in absorbing materials from its environment, and building them up into its own substance. From their point of view it can even be regarded as having an *aggressive* quality.

But we were not looking for the fundamental nature of aggression, but for the fundamental nature of anxiety, so we must now ask the questions: when does anxiety come into this most primitive function of life; and when it does arise should we regard it as arising from external or internal sources (if there is any difference between the two)? Of course, we cannot speak of ego anxiety or id anxiety until we have something resembling an ego or an id. Strictly speaking we have no right to talk of anxiety at all until there is some evidence of mind, but it is not the elaborations of anxiety that we are seeking (that is the sole content of the psychiatric textbooks), it is the fundamental nature of it; and to get to that perhaps it is best to start with an examination of life in its pre-anxiety state.

Is there anything resembling anxiety in the life process before mind, or the anatomical and physiological basis of mind, develops? It has been said by Reich (1942) that 'impulses and sensations are not created by the nerves, but are only transmitted by them. They are biological manifestations of the organism as a whole. They are present in the organism long before the development of an organized nervous tissue.' If this is true it may not be so absurd to consider whether an organism without a nervous system can experience anything comparable

THE FUNDAMENTAL NATURE OF ANXIETY

to anxiety. I have suggested[1] that when the amoeba has reached a certain stage of development consequent upon the process of growth, it might be regarded as being in a turgid or tense condition. (Biologists speak of an increasing 'turgor' in the growing cell.) At any rate there must be some change in it chemically or physically to initiate the process of cell division. We do not get an effect such as cell division without some cause. The condition of the overgrown amoeba must be regarded as containing the causes which bring about this subsequent division. Is there any difference between tension which is relieved by cell division, and tension, discomfort or perhaps even anxiety that is relieved by some behaviouristic or symptomatic phenomenon? May they not both share the honourable designation of id tension, or id anxiety?

However, I hope we are agreed, (i) that the characteristic process of life is that of growth including reproduction, and (ii) that this process must be in obedience to some physical, chemical, physiological or psychological urge or hunger, and (iii) that gratification, or something comparable to gratification, must lie in the successful fulfilment of this urge. Are we going to say that the whole nature of the life process is *altered* by the development of the specialized system, called the nervous system? And, if so, at what point in the course of its development, or evolution (from protoplasm, to neuro-motor apparatus, co-ordinated nerve fibres, network of nerve cells, autonomic nervous system or central nervous system) does this alteration or innovation take place? Does the fundamental nature of anxiety lie deeper than the level of so-called conscious mental activity? The fundamental nature of growth, of urges, and perhaps of gratifications, certainly does. And surely at these levels, too, frustration must occur. Frustration must mean that the living creature, or living substance, encounters a difficulty in the way of relieving the state of urge, tension, hunger or desire, brought into being chemically or physiologically. Anxiety may lie in the question as to whether or not it is going to overcome the frustration, or perhaps more primarily in the state of tension or discomfort due to unfulfilled urge or unneutralized chemical conditions, the relief of which the frustration is preventing.

[1] *Clinical Psychology*, Allen & Unwin, 1948, p. 61.

In this case we might postulate that an external danger, namely, the frustration, is experienced by the living substance or organism simply as an internal tension still unrelieved. So at a very early level of life we might suggest that the cause of anxiety, or failure to relieve tension, is due to an external cause (the frustrating object), but is experienced merely as an internal state, that of tension unrelieved and continuing to be unrelieved. Hence the distinction between an external danger and an internal danger would not exist before adequate ego development.

Having suggested that the primary behaviour of life is that of ingesting appropriate portions of its environment, presumably to relieve a chemically conditioned state of instability or tension, thereby achieving an enlargement, or growth, of its substance; and having suggested that this activity in itself entails some behaviouristic equivalent of self-assertion, or even of aggression, I would now suggest that the first reaction of a living organism to frustration would naturally be that of an exacerbation of this aggressive tendency. In seeking the fundamental nature of anxiety we seem to have suggested the fundamental nature of aggression *en route*. I doubt whether there is any need to postulate any other primary source or characteristic of aggression. In short, aggression is a phenomenon that emerges during the pursuit of chemically conditioned gratification and which is therefore naturally accentuated in the face of frustration.

In this connection I do not see the need to postulate a death-instinct. Surely all we can see on the primitive levels of life is a life-instinct, an instinct to absorb environment and grow, a process which entails self-assertion and aggression. Death comes with failure; but, before death, increasing tension or discomforture, with a heightening of aggressive urges, may be observable; and perhaps a point may be reached where something comparable to anxiety might be surmised, or even deduced. It may be that anxiety arises when a frustration cannot be overcome—and consequential death is imminent.

Why a death-instinct; Is it biologically or clinically inescapable? I would not like to suggest that I can disprove its existence. There are possibly some phenomena which this theory helps to integrate into the body of psychological knowledge, but when Melanie Klein says that 'Anxiety is aroused by the danger which threatens the organism from the *death-instinct'*, I wonder if she is justified, though I would not quarrel with her statement that 'Anxiety has its origin in the fear of death.' That is quite a different thing from the fear of a death-*instinct*. There is no doubt that anxiety may be felt as a result of an outraged and threatening super-ego; and with good reason, for it may, and occasionally does, destroy the individual. Suicide mostly, if not always, springs from this source. This is evidence of an aggressive super-ego, comparable to an aggressive parent or an aggressive state; but not evidence of a death-instinct.

SEXUAL FRUSTRATION AND ANXIETY

In pursuing our study of the infinitely complicated human mind, let us keep before us the principles suggested by this phylogenetic excursion.

Freud (1936, p. 124) says the first two danger situations which occasion anxiety, or anxiety-fixation, namely anxiety concerning loss of love and castration anxiety, have their source respectively in early childhood and in the phallic stage of libidinal development, however much they may be re-stimulated subsequently. It would seem that it is the third danger situation, namely, fear of the super-ego, more appropriate to the latency period, which is most continuously, or most obviously, stimulated throughout life. In a form of reaction to society, whether it is a projection of super-ego on to society, or introjection of society to reinforce super-ego, it is in frequent conflict with our unsublimated libidinal tendencies, pre-genital and genital.

Is it for that reason that our clinical experience presents us with libidinal frustration as the constant accompaniment of, if not source of, anxiety, and of neurotic and psycho-neurotic conditions? Evidence of frustrated aggression is, I think, less conspicuous clinically, and when it does arise it exhibits itself either reactively or in a suger-ego form, and then usually more as the frustrator than as the frustrated. My general impression is that the first reaction to frustration (usually libidinal frustration) would be aggression, or an exacerbation of already present aggression. If this reactive aggression is in turn frustrated or prevented, anxiety arises. In civilized communities then it appears to be in the field of sexuality in particular, that the life urge, or growth urge, is frustrated and prevented, to a large extent, from achieving a state of rest or of gratification.

Does anxiety arise in the ego as an ego-reaction to this observation of an external (or socially organized) frustration of the individual sexual instinct (with or without the complication of reactive and repressed aggression); or does it arise within the individual id in consequence of the frustration, external or internal, preventing sexual relief; or does it arise in the individual's ego as a reaction to a danger of tension from within, in the form of the sexual urge, threatening to overthrow the ego control and drive the individual into danger from society? Put another way, is it ego anxiety or id anxiety that is a reaction to sexual frustration, and if the former, does it arise as a reaction to the external frustration of society, or to the internal danger of the instinct threatening the ego's control? I would suggest that it may arise from every one of these sources and that they may all be most intimately related to one another. The differentiations arise only from the relative degree of accessibility to consciousness. Thus we see that such considerations tend to take us away from our main problem, namely, the *fundamental nature* of anxiety, instead of towards it.

An interesting contribution in the desired direction, suggesting a physiological origin of neurotic anxiety, has been made in a paper by Eeman (1949) elucidating the physiology of sexuality with particular reference to the orgasm. It is claimed that the work of the physiologists, Kuntz, White and Smithwick, on the autonomic nervous system has shown that sexual tumescence is a state of prolonged parasympatheticotonia, and that the phenomenon of detumescence, or orgasm, entails a sudden switchover to a brief, but very acute, sympatheticotonia. I think what is meant is that the phenomenon of orgasm is essentially a discharge of this sympatheticotonia.

I will not go into the interesting physiological details except to point out that according to Reich and, in different phraseology, Freud and others it is particularly a failure of adequate orgastic potency, especially if there is considerable sexual stimulation or parasympatheticotonia, which is responsible for the chronic sympatheticotonia of anxiety states. According to Eeman, Cannon's work on homoeostasis suggests that a healthy function of the autonomic nervous system, and presumably of life in general, necessitates a homoeostatic balance between para-sympatheticotonia and sympatheticotonia. Therefore, if we get the former, i.e. sexual stimulation, or tumescence, without a corresponding quantity of intensity of the latter, the missing discharge of the acute sympatheticotonia of orgasm is experienced by the individual as the chronic sympatheticotonia of the anxiety state. Eeman says: 'sympatheticotonia characteristic of the anxiety state is a failure of normal sympathetic discharge in orgasm'. If this is true, it would certainly be a contribution to Reich's theory, and in part a confirmation of his tenet that full orgastic potency and current orgastic discharge of tension is a *sine qua non* for health.

Thus we see that in attempting to reach the fundamental nature of anxiety, we are constantly approaching the frontiers of physiology, chemistry and physics. Let us return for a moment to Freud's position regarding this subject.

DESEXUALIZATION, ANXIETY AND EGO-BUILDING

In *Inhibitions, Symptoms and Anxiety*, Freud (1936, p. 150) says: 'Formerly I regarded anxiety as a general *reaction of the ego* to conditions of unpleasure. I always sought to account for its appearance on economic grounds, and I assumed, on the strength of my investigations into the actual neuroses, that libido (sexual excitement) which was rejected or not utilized by the ego found *direct discharge* in the form of anxiety. It cannot be denied that these various assertions did not go very well together, or at any rate did not imply one another. Moreover, they gave the impression of there being a specially intimate connection between anxiety and libido, and this did not accord with the general character of anxiety as a reaction to unpleasure . . . Thus it is a question of id-anxiety (instinctual anxiety) versus ego-anxiety. Since the energy which the ego employed is desexualized, the new view tended to weaken the close connection between anxiety and libido. I hope I have at least succeeded in making the contradiction plain and in giving a clear idea of the point in doubt.' (My italics.)

The thought that came to my mind here was this: perhaps 'desexualized' *means* anxiety. The life process is a process of relieving tension, gratifying hunger. The energy of the life instinct responsible for this process is regarded by Freud as libidinal, sexual (though not necessarily genital). He here mentions that the energy which the ego employs is desexualized, that is to say, presumably no longer gratifying, or pleasurable. This renunciation of pleasure, this desexualization, is, I believe, rendered possible only through fear, that is to say, in response to danger. If the danger becomes a menace to life, sensed by the organism as a frustration which its aggression does not readily overcome, pleasure no longer exists and every bit of its available energy, aggression and everything else has to be utilized to deal with the interrupting (frustrating) situation that menaces its gratification, and hence menaces the chemico-physical basis of its life—though it may only sense it in the form of a persistent frustration to gratification (i.e. to a neutralization of the chemico-physical tension engendered by the life process). In other words, I would suggest that anxiety could be regarded as desexualization in process. But it is more than this. It is the only thing that causes the organism to give up its pleasure-seeking, its pleasure principle, its internal id-life of gratification (because it is no longer achieving it) and to take cognizance of interfering reality. (Cf. McDougall's definition of anxiety already quoted.)

Therefore I would say, that, like reality, specifically interfering or gratification-withholding reality, *anxiety* is the ego-builder.

Ego building, or ego development, the fruit of desexualization, is perhaps only possible through the castrating effect of reality dangers. Because, unless the organism develops an ego to deal with reality, it will not overcome the frustration and will in consequence die (as a result of the accumulation of unrelieved chemico-physical tension). At levels lower than the human, or even at the human level, the ego need not know anything of this. Perhaps even organisms without an ego 'become aware' of something internal in the form of accumulating tension which they cannot relieve. I would here say that when an animal (or human) becomes exasperated or frantic (traumatic state), it means that he can endure his tension no longer. He is rightly frantic (like a man being suffocated), for this intolerability means the sensing from within of impending death.

I would suggest that what Freud thought was confusion between his contradictory theories of libido being transformed

THE FUNDAMENTAL NATURE OF ANXIETY

into anxiety and anxiety emanating from the ego as a signal of external or internal danger becomes clarification if we go down to the lower (or pre-ego) levels of life. At those levels they are all one and the same thing. External danger or frustration need not be sensed by the primitive organism as such—nor, indeed, as anything external at all. It causes a rising of tension within the organism—a rising of chemico-physical tension, with or without a psychological apperception thereof. And the only thing the organism becomes aware of (if it 'becomes aware' of anything) is this rising tension. This is identical with anxiety, though it is an internal experience—caused by an external frustration. The earliest sense of reality in primitive life, and perhaps in all life, is a sensing of its effect upon the organism's internal state. Whichever way a frustration is sensed, and certainly once there is a clue that there is something in the environment causing it, the resulting tension demands that the organism gives all it has in the form of attention to reality, that is to say, demands that it forms an ego. Why else should it abandon the pleasure-principle? Otherwise why should the libido be desexualized—except under the lash of reality fear? In other words, it may be that anxiety is the experiencing of the actual process of desexualizing libido—a castrating process, a process which can take place only (a) under the whip of reality danger and (b) under the whip of unprojected realities in the form of the super-ego-suggesting, phantasying, or threatening danger. Once such a process has started the ego may well make further inroads upon the pleasure-principle and by this desexualization continue to be built up or to build itself up.

I am suggesting that a reality sense as we would understand the term, i.e. an ego, only arises when reality frustrates the automatic gratification or pleasure-principle of the chemically based life process of growth and reproduction. And further, that anxiety is the affect experienced during the interruption or frustration of the pleasure-gratifying life process. It is a condition in which all the energy resources of the organism are deflected from their pleasure-seeking aim, desexualized and handed over to whatever ego there is to give it energy and power to deal with external reality.

I think this may clarify an early situation in the course of phylogenetic development. Many phenomena may be observed in support of this thesis. For instance, such large phenomena as the evolution of *Homo sapiens* from his *biologically better placed* progenitors; the relatively greater ego development of this species in the niggardly environment of temperate zones as compared with the tropical zones, e.g. Central Africa; and such minor questions as to whether the Jews (or some of them) have become extra intelligent through racial (phylogenetic) fear, etc.

To attempt further clarification of our main concept: anxiety and ego-building, or in the first instance ego-creation, go hand in hand, and I suggest that their material basis is the chemico-physical condition that arises in an organism and that primarily gives rise to an urge, hunger or desire. When reality frustrates a 'neutralization' of this accumulated chemico-physical condition (frustration of gratification of the desire), the chemico-physical condition giving rise to the hunger or desire persists and continuing discomfort (tension), instead of the pleasure of relief, is experienced.

This discomfort or tension is, in my opinion, identical with a state of anxiety, particularly or conspicuously if it becomes accentuated and persistent. It leads to an abandonment by the organism of the pleasurable principle (already inoperative on account of frustration) and an automatic mobilization of all the resources of the organism, all its energies, to deal with the cause of the frustration. This commonly means a concentration of attention upon reality, frustrating reality. It is just this cognizance of reality and manipulation of it which are the characteristic of ego function. The first instances of this in phylogeny and development, accompanied as they must be by abandonment (at least temporarily) of the pleasure principle and by experience of the antithetical feeling of anxiety, are the first signs of ego function. From this the ego comes into being, and, at the instigation of further reality frustrations, it develops. As instinct gratification is accompanied by pleasure, this process of instinct frustration and ego development is accompanied by anxiety. The degree of anxiety will naturally vary from imperceptible faintness when the ego is in process of successfully coping with reality and removing frustrating obstacles to instinct gratification, to heightening tension when the ego is failing and frustration persisting.

These are descriptions of early mental mechanisms only,

before further psychic development masks or confuses the simplicity of the early picture, and hides the fundamental nature of anxiety in a maze of developmental elaborations. Thus the antithesis which I have suggested is not the familiar one of life-instinct and death-instinct, but one more in keeping, I think, with out clinical experience, namely, the antithesis between instinct gratification and anxiety. Anxiety is the experience of tension, unpleasure or pain that arises when gratification is frustrated and fails. Its normal effect is to create a new distribution of energy to deal with the frustration, a reality factor, an ego. And so the ego is born and develops out of the pain of frustration, the desexualization of libidinal energy. *The antithesis between instinct and anxiety becomes the antithesis between id and ego.*

As an organism becomes more complex the reactions of the primitive ego to external frustrations and dangers become vastly complicated by its having to turn its attention to states of instinct tension which would threaten its freedom from within. It may well be torn between the contrary problems of adapting reality to suit its instinct demands, and in suppressing its instinct demands when these would endanger its relationship to reality. The position is made still more complicated bv the existence of the super-ego (introjected parents, together with the endophysic factor) which must also be placated in the course of ego adjustment. From this complex situation of three variables, and the frustrations and anxieties contingent upon their adaptation, all the infinite material psychopathology has been built up. I have merely attempted, though perhaps not very successfully, to avoid getting lost in this limitless maze in favour of an endeavour to turn our attention to where we came in.[1]

---

[1] Following further reflections on the theme of this paper, I suggest this definition:

Anxiety is a state of tension that arises in an organism in consequence of frustration of instinct gratification (cf. un-neutralised chemico-physical metabolic changes), and subsequently in anticipation of this. It marks interruption of the operation of the pleasure-principle and inauguration of the reality-principle or ego. With the development of ego-nuclei anxiety may be regarded as basically an id-tension which can emerge into consciousness directly, and also indirectly via functional somatic discharges.

After the development of psychic structure, anxiety also arises in the ego as a danger signal in anticipation of ego frustration, or overthrow, from three possible sources: (1) uncontrollable pressure of id-tension; (2) reality danger; and (3) superego disapproval.

Clinically, anxiety is commonly seen in consequence of erotic stimulation with relatively little relief, inhibited or inadequate orgasm often leaving some undischarged tension.

The first part of this definition is in keeping with Freud's original idea that frustrated libido was transformed into anxiety; and the second part corresponds to his later theory that anxiety arises in the ego as a signal of anticipated danger from the pressure of unrelieved id-tension.

The second aspect of anxiety, according to what I have written, is impossible until after the development of psychic structure. It therefore has little or nothing to do with the *fundamental* nature of anxiety, which I have regarded as pre-dating the development of such structure and in fact giving rise to it.

REFERENCES

Berg, C. (1948). *Clinical Psychology*, p. 61. London: Allen and Unwin.

Bleuler, E. (1930). *Textbook of Psychiatry* (translated by A. A. Brill). New York: The Macmillan Company.

Eeman, P. D. (1949). Physiology of the orgasm and of psychoanalysis. *Int. J. Sexology.* 3, 92-8.

Fenichel, O. (1946). *The Psychoanalytic Theory of Neurosis.* London: Kegan Paul, Trench, Trubner and Co. Ltd.

Freud, S. (1933). *New Introductory Lectures on Psycho-Analysis.* London: Hogarth Press and Institute of Psycho-Analysis.

Freud, S. (1936). *Inhibitions, Symptoms and Anxiety.* London: Hogarth Press and Institute of Psycho-Analysis.

Hinsie, L. E. and Shatzky, J. (1940). *Psychiatric Dictionary.* New York: Oxford University Press.

Klein, M. (1932). *The Psycho-Analysis of Children*, pp. 183-4. London: Hogarth Press and Institute of Psycho-Analysis.

Klein, M. (1948). A contribution to the theory of anxiety and guilt. *Int. J. Psycho-Anal.* 29, 114.

McDougall W. (1926). *Outline of Abnormal Psychology.* New York: Charles Scribner's Sons.

Rank, O. (1929). *The Trauma of Birth*, pp. 11, 12 ff. London: Kegan Paul, Trench, Trubner and Co. Ltd.

Reich, W. (1942). *The Function of the Orgasm*, pp. 255-6 (translated by T. P. Wolfe). New York: Orgone Institute Press.

IV

Fear—Normal and Abnormal

(1)

The psychological importance of fear cannot be overestimated. There is much to indicate that it is practically the most important of all mental phenomena. For one thing it takes priority of attention and urgency over all other emotions. Further, it is admitted by most psychologists that it is the foundation or cause of nearly all mental and nervous disorders. Some would go further and suggest that most physical disorders, even organic diseases, owe their initial cause to fear or to morbid anxiety.

The difference between normal fear and abnormal (commonly called 'morbid anxiety') would seem at first sight to be apparent. It is generally assumed that the former is entirely due to an external stimulus, while the cause, or source, of the latter is quite unseen and perhaps unseeable. Freud (1936) says: 'In precise speech we use the word "fear" rather than "anxiety" if the feeling has found an object . . . objective danger is a danger that is known and objective anxiety is anxiety about a known danger of this sort. Neurotic anxiety is anxiety about an unknown danger. Neurotic danger is thus a danger that has still to be discovered. Analysis has shown that it is an instinctual danger.'

He goes on to say: 'In some cases the characteristics of objective anxiety and neurotic anxiety are mingled. The danger is known and objective but the anxiety in regard to it is over-great, greater than seems proper. It is this surplus of anxiety which betrays the presence of a neurotic element. Such cases, however, contain no new principle; for analysis shows that to the known objective danger is attached an unknown instinctual one.'

Thus it will be seen that the distinction between normal and abnormal fear cannot always be sharply defined. Even in normal fear there is considerable evidence to suggest that the outer danger is commonly reacted to excessively only because it resonates, as it were, with one operating inside us.

I have tried to make this aetiological distinction between the two kinds of fear vivid by saying that normal fear is fear of the tiger *outside* and abnormal fear of the tiger *inside* us. Nevertheless, it seems we would not be afraid of the tiger outside unless we had one inside us which we had learnt to fear. It has been called in question by some psychologists as to whether fear can be experienced at all unless it arouses something in the unconscious mind of the experiencing organism, something which is a complex, that is to say, a repressed morbid anxiety rather than any rational estimation of real danger.[1]

To pass from aetiology to manifestations or symptomatology; from whatever source it *arises*, fear has both mental and physical *manifestations*. The physical manifestations are, indeed, so abundant that once there was a theory, now called the James-Lange theory, which held that the experience of fear consisted in nothing more than sensations arriving in consciousness, from the physical reactions. However, I think we would all agree nowadays that the essence of fear is mental as well as physical, even if the two cannot clearly be separated.

Mental Manifestations of Fear

We all consciously appreciate the affective tone of fear; the attention is fixed and concentrated on the disturbing object, and all other stimuli are inhibited. Perception, sensation and consciousness are abnormally acute. The entire mental apparatus is toned up to its most extreme powers, involving all its relevant functions. There is evidence that something [which Crile (1917) thought was iodized protein from the thyroid] has facilitated the passage of electrical currents through the semi-permeable membranes of the synapses in the nervous system and so lowered the threshold to all stimuli. We certainly get physical as well as mental phenomena suggestive of some such happening; for instance, the increased muscular as well as the increased mental tone.

[1] Freud says that in the study of small children there is nothing that leads him to believe that there is any such thing as 'an instinctive perception of externally threatening danger'. It is true, he says, that external circumstances may combine with internal or endogenous fears, but the latter are primary. He further adds that there are three practically universal childhood fears that 'may be termed almost normal'; they are the fear of being alone, the fear of strangers, and the fear of darkness, each of which is associated with the unconscious dread of losing the protecting influences of the mother.

Physical Manifestations of Fear

These normally include a mobilizing of all the resources of the organism for appropriate action. As Cannon (1929) puts it, the balance between the sympathetic and parasympathetic divisions of the autonomic nervous system is disturbed in favour of the sympathetic. In short, energy seems to be withdrawn from the parasympathetic and poured into the sympathetic nervous system. All organs and glands normally subject to the double innervation are intensely stimulated. Practically every system and organ of the body is affected: the sphincters of the alimentary canal contract; the viscera dilate; digestion ceases; and blood leaves the abdominal organs and is driven by vasomotor action to the parts of the body where it is in urgent demand—the brain, the central nervous system, the heart, voluntary musculature and the lungs. There is subsequently dilatation of the pupil, proptosis and widening of the palpabral fissure. Owing to stimulation of the sympathetic, adrenalin is poured into the blood-stream, the glycogen of the liver is transformed into sugar which circulates freely in the dilated arterioles of the musculature, supplying it with the necessary fuel for sustained action. At the same time, the blood is caused to coagulate more rapidly (which has its use in the event of wounds), the heart beat is intensely accelerated, and the respiration increased in depth and frequency. The muscle tone is so much increased that, unless physical activity ensues, tremor is liable to take place.

No doubt a host of further physical manifestations could be tabulated, but perhaps enough has been said to indicate that fear mobilizes all the resources of the organism for the expenditure of energy, presumably to meet the exigencies of a danger situation. A cat can leap ten times as far in a state of fear. It was said of Mademoiselle Lenglen that unless she was actually trembling before an important tennis match she knew she would not win. Once on court the trembling was transformed into the activity and vitality which made her a champion.

Morbid Anxiety

As regards *manifestations,* the essential difference between the phenomenon of normal fear and the symptoms of morbid anxiety is that whereas in fear practically all the mental and physical symptoms described are present in a related or comparable degree, in morbid anxiety, on the other hand, any one or more of these symptoms may stand out in striking disproportion to the others. For example, a person suffering from morbid anxiety may complain merely of an unpleasant feeling of mental apprehension without any of its physical accompaniments, or at least without their being observed. In contradistinction to this, he may present himself with a single physical symptom, such as tachycardia, sometimes without any mental accompaniment. It is, of course, a little more usual for several symptoms to be combined, though the combination may be quite disproportionate to that encountered in normal fear. These symptoms, single or combined, can be legion. They can be classified under every system, organ and function of the human body.

Regarding the *mental* symptoms, it may be said that almost the whole of psychiatric symptomatology might be written if we pursued morbid anxiety into every nook and cranny of nervous and mental illness.

Even the *physical* symptoms of anxiety we could not here find space to tabulate in full. For instance, they can be *sensory*, such as hyperaesthesiae, anaesthesiae and particularly paraesthesiae; *muscular*—paralysis, paresis, or local spasms, tics, tremors and even fits. Perhaps the commonest phenomena under this heading include a generalized state of muscular tension, often escaping observation, and local spasms, or semi-spasms, often responsible for chronic aches and pains; for instance, backache simulating lumbago or fibrositis.

The *special senses* are not immune, disturbance of the eyes ranging from hyperacuity to total functional blindness. Hearing also can range from hyperacuity to total deafness. Disorders of taste and smell are common. The *skin* is almost invariably affected in severe cases, from coldness or blueness to excessive perspiration, particularly in local areas such as the palms of the hands. Disorders of balance occur more often than not.

Amongst the physical *functions*, the *sexual function* is probably the most consistently disordered. In males, the disorders here include impotence, *ejaculatio praecox* and almost every form and degree of too quick or unsatisfactory coitus. In the female, the outstanding symptoms are vaginismus, dyspareunia and frigidity, or orgastic frigidity. Disorders of *speech* include aphonia and stammer.

Under the *cardiovascular system* we have the common disorders of tachycardia, irregularity and pseudo-angina. Vasomotor disorders include blushings, sweatings, coldness of extremities, and, I would add, Raynaud's phenomenon and even thrombo-angiitis obliterans.

Under the *respiratory system* we have disturbances such as feelings of suffocation—from which the term 'anxiety' derives its name—as well as dyspnoea, asthma and others. Under the *digestive system* the number of symptoms is legion, ranging from mild abdominal discomforts and nervous dyspepsia to constipation, diarrhoea and vomiting, distensions, flatulence, anorexia, spastic colon and proctalgia fugax. Even the *urinary system* is not free from some expression of anxiety, from functional anuria (many men cannot urinate in a public urinal) to the even more common polyuria.

The above are all common accompaniments of morbid anxiety, but there can be an almost imperceptible transition from normal fear reactions to abnormal, or at any rate injurious reactions. This fear mechanism was no doubt very useful in the forest, and indeed essential for survival when the difference between life and death depended upon flight, fight, or the third possible defensive measure, namely, immobilization (sometimes called 'freezing'), but in the environment of civilization the old reaction patterns are not always suitable. Excessive sugar in the blood may be essential for flight or fight, but it can be a potential danger when neither activity is undertaken. Hence, as the late Sir Walter Langdon-Brown used to say: 'When stocks go down in New York, diabetes goes up.'

It is conceivable that a frequent or almost constant experience of 'normal' fear, particularly in very early life, will cause a *facilitation* of fear reactions with all the illness-producing consequences of such a facilitation. Some would say it is as though a sort of engram, or channel, were built thereby in the nervous system through which subsequent stimuli would end to flow. In other words, the anxiety might then become a habit and lead to chronic physical and nervous exhaustion.

In practice, however, we more commonly come across illnesses resulting from the constant stimulation of morbid anxiety whether or not this is precipitated or accentuated by any external, real danger situation. We rarely encounter illness resulting from the effects of real danger *per se*. Experience teaches us to blame the more constant stimulus of anxiety arising from internal or unconscious sources. There is little doubt that such excess of anxiety may lead not only to physical and nervous exhaustion, but that illness, mental, psychoneurotic and organic, of practically every variety, not excluding accidents, may be initiated. It is not too much to say that even death may ensue—either directly through exhaustion, e.g. cardiac exhaustion, or indirectly through a lowering of the resistances to infection or to some other noxious or morbid process—a reflection of the utmost importance for medicine, or for its predicted successor, psychosomatic medicine. We shall consider these sequelae of anxiety in the second part of this paper.

(2)

Psychogenic Illness

The illnesses which arise from fear, normal and abnormal—and it is doubtful whether any, even accidents, can be excluded—may be divided into those connected with its mental and those connected with its physical manifestations.

The former comprise practically the whole of psychiatry, and the latter have been said by the enthusiasts of psychosomatic medicine to be destined, if traced to their uttermost ramifications, to comprise almost the whole of organic medicine! Be this as it may, the important thing for us as doctors is not only this distressing state of morbid anxiety, but more particularly the innumerable psychological and physical, and even organic, consequences which undoubtedly can and do ensue. I shall tabulate these briefly, and refer to their mechanisms in order of their proximity to the original and initiating fear reactions.

To begin with, the *mental* side of the picture: the physical manifestations of morbid anxiety which we have been following may be regarded as a mechanism for the discharge of *mental* tension. The mind itself has recourse to other measures also in its endeavours to deal with excessive excitation. One of these is the *blocking* of stimuli, preventing them from entering. The mental apparatus has its limits in its ability to cope with stimuli both from outside and from inside. The process of blocking may range from simple inattention to the less familiar one of loss of consciousness. This is obviously a total blocking of all stimulation as a mechanism of self-preservation on the part of the mental apparatus. This corresponds to one aspect of Freud's 'primal repression'.[1]

There are many other mechanisms at work. In fact, we might stretch this statement a little and include under this heading practically every mental (and physical) phenomenon, behaviouristic and otherwise. They are all ways of coping with tensions introduced into, or arising out of, the mental apparatus.

Next in the list of such mechanisms we should perhaps include the phenomenon of 'binding'.[2] It would seem that stimuli if they do penetrate the first defences, such as those of inattention or blocking, and are a bit excessive, or unwanted by the mind at the moment, create tensions which are, as it were, put aside or repressed so that they do not interfere with the particular activity in hand at the moment. However, there is evidence that these bound excitations still reside somewhere in the mental apparatus, and are liable subsequently to show their presence by emerging when the repressing forces relax, and cause tensions and anxieties. Phobia formation could be regarded as a device on the part of the mental apparatus to bind free-floating anxiety tensions by means of a concept or idea, thereby leaving the rest of the mental apparatus free from very disturbing influences. Similarly, most symptom-formation could be thus regarded. *Symptoms are not so much an illness as they are a sign of the measures which the mind has taken to deal with interfering excitations and tensions in order that it should be as far as possible free to cope with reality and the needs of the organism.*

A phenomenon in this category which is commonly ignored, and is perhaps the most important of all, is the phenomenon of *character formation.* The formation of character is no doubt the most difficult aspect of the end products which result in the mind in the course of its endeavour to bind undue excitations and to protect itself against disturbing anxieties.

Although psychogenic illnesses are, generally speaking, indirectly bound up with the patient's character, unless we are analysts or psycho-therapists we had best content ourselves with

---

[1] *Vide* Brierley (1951).

[2] This term is not used sufficiently in the literature, although Freud (1920) elucidated the concept. It would seem that the more comprehensive term 'repression' has replaced it.

the more superficial aspects or pathological manifestations that emerge and can more definitely be called illness. Presently I shall try to elucidate the mechanism of the most common physical ones. In the meantime I shall refer to some of the *psychological* sequelae of anxiety.

First there is the *anxiety state* itself. I still think that Freud's original classification is the best. He divided symptoms of morbid anxiety into two principal categories. The first he called anxiety neurosis, which he regarded as arising from factors in the current sexual life of the patient in a pure form, not necessarily having any contributory element from the psychology of the patient. According to Freud, the pathology of this anxiety condition was essentially the arousing or mobilization of sexual excitement (i.e. tumescence) with inadequate detumescence. The tensions thus aroused and undischarged were first said by Freud to become 'transformed' into the affect of anxiety. Subsequently he changed his theory in favour of the idea that the *ego*, which has to keep control over instinct drives, reacted with anxiety when the undischarged sexual tension was so great as to seem to threaten ego control.

The other major anxiety illness Freud called *anxiety hysteria*. The distinguishing feature of this was that anxiety was not necessarily caused by current factors, but rather by repressed complexes going right back to the childhood experiences of the patient. Here the anxiety was largely a reaction on the part of the ego to the repressed tensions connected with infantile traumata. In practice, these two illnesses are almost invariably combined, and thus the usual term nowadays for a psychogenic state of anxiety is *anxiety state,* implying both anxiety neurosis and anxiety hysteria.

Anxiety hysteria may develop into the more typical form of hysteria called conversion hysteria. The characteristic of this is that the anxiety is 'converted' into physical symptoms. The mechanism of conversion here requires explanation, not only on account of its importance for an understanding of hysteria and other psychoneuroses, but also in order to distinguish it clearly from the mechanisms of vegetative neuroses and of organ neuroses (psychosomatic diseases) which we shall presently endeavour to clarify. Now please read the following paragraph very slowly and carefully as it is important fully to understand

this concept so characteristic of psychoneurotic symptomatology.

Conversion

When we are stimulated from either without or within in a
specific way, the result is the arousing within us of both a
specific emotion and a specific form of behaviour. So far everything is normal; we act in a certain way in response to the
stimulation from without and from within. Behaviour means
purposeful action in which voluntary muscles and our sensory
perceptive systems are involved. Thus there is nothing
mysterious about a psychological state being 'converted' into a
physical state or a physical activity. It is, in fact, the *essence* of
the behaviour of a living organism, or at least of a living
organism that has a mind, i.e. *mental phenomena are converted
into physical phenomena whenever we move, whenever we do
anything.* Now, when the emotion aroused is unwanted by the
ego and repressed from consciousness, it can, and in some persons does, gain an expression of its feeling and of its purpose
independently of the conscious levels of the mind which will
not admit it. Such an expression is always a symbolic substitute
for the emotional wish or desire. It is almost as if a separate
personality were acting independently of the main personality.
The characteristic of a *conversion* symptom is, however, that it
is active in a manner analogous to that of ordinary behaviour.
An amusing example of this was the case of a man patient of
mine whose legs gave way on every occasion when he was proceeding to church to marry his fiancée!

Bodily behaviour, whether of muscles or of organs, which is
independent of the person's integrated ego, speaks, as it were, a
language of its own (cf. 'organ language'), usually symbolical of
some repudiated wish. It can be understood only by interpreta-
tion of that symbolical language. It is the conversion of a *dis-
owned* wish into behaviour that is outside that of the organized
ego.

Illness Arising from the Physical Accompaniments of Anxiety
*From the physical accompaniments of a constant or excessive
state of anxiety there arises in gradations of severity a succession
of symptoms and diseases.*

The first series of these has been given the name of the *vegeta-*

tive neuroses. In the same way that an understanding of conversion was important for psychoneurotic symptomatology, so a thorough understanding of the mechanism of the production of vegetative neuroses is important for the understanding of the psychogenesis of physical illness. The psychogenesis of symptoms coming under this heading is almost apparent once we have accepted the inescapable fact that somatic changes invariably accompany every emotion and every emotionally charged idea. Whether we consider fear or rage or any other emotion, we cannot escape the fact that it invariably has *physiological accompaniments.* If severe, these can in themselves amount to an illness although they are only *affect equivalents.* In the case of fear we have enumerated a host of these embracing nearly every system of the body. *Vegetative neuroses* are not substitute expressions of repressed emotions such as we get in conversion hysteria; *they are accentuations of the normal physiological accompaniments of the emotion* (Alexander, 1943). It is the *chronicity* of emotional tension which makes the condition morbid. For instance, if a person is continually in a state of morbid anxiety he is liable to suffer from various *symptoms* of normal fear. For example, undue sweating, sometimes local rather than general. The secretions of his stomach juices will probably be altered. The skin also is a vegetative organ, and many skin troubles would be rightly classified under vegetative neuroses. Psychogenic urticarias are vegetative neuroses, but it would be right to say that these skin reactions have passed beyond the category of affect equivalents. Some disorders are a combination of vegetative neuroses and conversion mechanism (already described). For instance, sphincter troubles, including constipation and diarrhoea and bladder dysfunctions. Blushing is said to be more of a conversion symptom. In short, vegetative neuroses are the first morbid result of the chronic expression of some somatic disturbance *normally present when a particular emotion is aroused.*

Organ neuroses (sometimes called psychosomatic illnesses) come under another category. According to Alexander, they are neither vegetative neuroses nor conversion symptoms. They are, on the other hand, a somatic *end-result* of a long-standing psychogenic disturbance. For instance, if a person in a state of anxiety has his gastric juices altered and the functional movements of his stomach arrested in accordance with the physiological mechanisms of fear, though the alteration in his gastric juices, etc., would come under the category of vegetative neuroses, as this is the physiological accompaniment of his morbid state of fear, the peptic ulcer that may eventually ensue is neither a vegetative neurosis nor a conversion symptom; it is the *result* of the effect upon his stomach of stasis and alterations of secretion and function.

We have thus proceeded, in stages, from fear to actual organic disease and thus entered what is perhaps a fairly new field of medical research, the importance of which cannot, I think, be over-estimated.

This fact will be better appreciated if I mention that, according to Dunbar (1943) statistics show that the commonest of all organic illnesses is cardiovascular disease (including hypertension), classed by her as psychosomatic. It accounts for twelve per cent of invalidism in the U.S.A., second only to nervous and mental causes of invalidism (eighteen per cent). Rheumatism, with rheumatoid arthritis, another psychosomatic disease, is a close second. According to some authorities other important and common psychosomatic illnesses include gastroduodenal disorders and diseases, including ulcer; intestinal, including constipation and colitis; allergies, including hay fever, asthma, the common cold and sinusitis; respiratory disorders and diseases, including bronchitis and even psychologically-initiated phthisis; endocrine disorders, including thyrotoxicosis, metabolic disorders and diabetes; skin reactions and diseases, including urticaria, pruritus, dermatitis, and most others; vasomotor and blood diseases, including anaemia; migraine; some epilepsies; disorders of renal function; accidents; and, of course, effort intolerance, sometimes called effort syndrome.

There are even some enthusiasts who believe that every organic disease (not excepting cancer!) has, like those we have just enumerated, its source or initial origin in the psyche. Time and research may prove. There can be no doubt, however, that in the meantime the concept of psychogenesis has come to stay.

(3)

I have tried to clarify the relationship between the *mental* attributes of *anxiety* and such defensive and symptomatic reactions as *character formation, anxiety state* and *conversion symptoms;* also the relationship between the *physical* accompaniments of emotion, *vegetative neuroses* and *psychogenic organic disease.* These matters are very relevant to our subject because, although some diseases are attributed to other emotions (for instance, essential hypertension to chronic, repressed rage), there is little doubt that the main factor in all psychogenic illnesses is anxiety, with its inseparable physiological and somatic changes.

We have traced in outline the operation of anxiety in the production of various mental and physical illnesses. It remains only to return to our nuclear symptom, anxiety, and to trace this phenomenon in *the other direction* to see if we can learn something of the fundamental source and nature of anxiety itself.

Here we shall see its true relationship, indeed its identity, with normal fear. Fear arises when the autonomy of the organism is threatened. This is tantamount to saying: when instinct gratification is prevented by some frustration from without or from within. Phylogenetically, this frustration was originally from without. Hence fear was originally normal fear. Morbid anxiety became possible only after the elaboration of psychic structure.

I think I can best clarify the position if I begin with the conception of the phylogenetic origin and development of anxiety which I have previously given. Even in the most primitive organism, metabolism gives rise to certain chemico-physical changes, the organism's behaviour being stimulated by these changes towards an alteration or neutralization of them. On the analogy of instinct gratification it was suggested that this was an automatic process which sooner or later in the course of evolution might be regarded as subserving the pleasure principle. I went on to say that if this process were frustrated by some external agent (e.g. the absence of food) and the organism therefore failed even temporarily to neutralize the chemico-physical condition somatically produced, it would thereupon experience an increasing discomfiture or tension. The frustration therefore would terminate the operation of the pleasure principle and would lead instead to a condition of tension indistinguishable from anxiety.

I went on to say that it was only such a state of tension or anxiety that, having caused the organism to cease operating under the pleasure principle, forced it to attend to the frustrating reality and thereby inaugurated the birth of the reality principle or ego. Without the development of such a reality principle or ego it would fail to deal successfully with its frustrations, the injurious chemico-physical condition would increase and the organism would die.

Thus I gave anxiety a fundamental position in biological survival and in the inauguration and development, in due course, of psychic structure. With this development alterations naturally ensue. Amongst the first of these one might place the power of *anticipating* such a frustrating and potentially damaging or annihilating situation before it actually arose. The phenomenon of abnormal anxiety is closely related to these alterations. The ego, having come into existence and being the integrating and executive factor in the mind, is in a position not only to become directly aware of internal discomfort due to frustrations and consequent instinct tensions, and is not only capable of anticipating the event of these, but is also capable of anticipating situations in which its own power of control, both of the external and of the internal world, may be threatened. It both senses and anticipates the tiger both within and without. Hence its potentiality for anxiety reaction is only too understandable.

Failure to neutralize a chemico-physical condition metabolically induced, that is to say, inability to satisfy one's need or to gratify one's instinct, may well be the first step towards death. This condition is identical with one of discomfort, tension, anxiety. All the potentialities and energies of the organism are mobilized for relief and survival.

Short of death, partial failure produces illnesses—which may be regarded as partial death—mental and physical illnesses. These illnesses, which were originally produced by an external agent, or rather by the organism's failure to react adequately to an external agent, can in the course of psychological evolution proceed from the organisms' failure to deal appropriately with conflicts and tensions within its own psyche; in short, they can proceed from intrapsychic morbidity, the first manifestation of which is abnormal fear or morbid anxiety.

REFERENCES

Alexander, Franz (1943). *Psychosomatic Medicine,* Vol. V, No. 3, pp. 208-9.

Berg, Charles (1948). *Clinical Psychology,* Ch. 6. London: Allen and Unwin.

Brierley, Marjorie (1951). *Trends in Psycho-Analysis,* p. 31.

Cannon, W. B. (1929). *Bodily Changes in Pain, Hunger, Fear and Rage.* New York: Appleton.

Crile, G. W. (1917). *Man, an Adaptive Mechanism.* New York: Macmillan.

Dunbar, Flanders (1943). *Psychosomatic Medicine,* pp. 18, 19. New York: Paul B. Hoeber.

Freud, S. (1920). *Beyond the Pleasure Principle,* pp. 30, 34-7, 39, 42, 44, 80-2.

Freud, S. (1936). *Inhibitions, Symptoms and Anxiety,* pp. 158, 159, 160.

V

A Note on the Author

by

CLIFFORD ALLEN, M.D.

I first met Charles Berg some twenty-six years ago, quite casually, at the Tavistock Clinic where we were both working. He was waiting for someone else when I came in and we entered into conversation. I did not know who he was then, but from the first he impressed me, not only by his looks, but by his pleasant and charming manner. After talking for a few minutes I appreciated that he was immensely erudite, and knew much more about psychotherapy than I did. Yet his talk was casual and he never made any attempt to impress anyone.

He was a tall, well-built man with black hair, dark sparkling eyes and a humorous mouth. It was obvious that he looked at life with a tolerant, kindly attitude, and that nothing disturbed his amused, quizzical outlook. He applied to his less experienced colleagues his tolerance but saw clearly enough where they failed in technique. Some of his remarks were critical but in all the years I knew him he never said anything cruel or unkind about anyone. He was capable of considerable wit but never as a weapon.

Berg often attended meetings at the Tavistock Clinic. These meetings at that time were sort of endemic and those on the staff were expected to attend constantly. Unfortunately many of those who spoke produced more words than ideas. Even though he listened with quiet amusement Berg never did more than shrug his shoulders; although had he wished he could have demolished many a speaker's reputation. When he spoke he had a quiet confidence, merely expressing his disagreement whilst putting forward his much more fundamental and constructive views.

He rarely spoke about himself: it was not until years later that I knew that he had been born in India and had had such a cosmopolitan youth; attended various schools in India, London and Lausanne in Switzerland. His father had been a man who found it difficult to stay in one place and so the family had constantly moved about from one country to another.

One might have expected that such a varied existence would have led to a young man developing a superficial manner which gave him savoir faire but no depth. Such was certainly not true of Berg. Although he had savoir faire he was cultured and fundamentally a scholar. In fact, seeing how hard he worked with his patients, it was remarkable how much he managed to read.

He trained medically at St. Thomas's Hospital but before he could qualify the First World War broke out. At first he served as a Surgeon Probationer on hospital ships until 1915, when he was released to obtain his medical qualification — M.R.C.S., L.R.C.P. This he did easily, and was then lent to the hospital to act as Casualty Officer and Resident Anaesthetist.

Six months later he was working in Bombay as a Surgical Specialist. It is probable that he was given this position on the principle that in the Army it was then usual to allot specialities to anyone available, without reference to qualifications or experience. Berg never made any pretence of liking surgery and, in fact, later came to detest it.

After the war finished he returned to St. Thomas's Hospital and worked at the York Road Lying-In Hospital, where he took his final M.B., B.S. examination. He then prepared himself for general practice (to which he then thought he would devote his life) by working as a locum tenens. This he enjoyed but came to feel in time that he was getting nowhere. It was not curing coughs and indigestion that interested him, but the vast mass of neurotic patients who returned again and again because no one discovered the emotional disturbances which lay behind their symptoms.

One might divide general practitioners into two classes. There are those who close their minds to the possibility that illness is caused by anything other than organic factors — bacteria, injuries, toxins and so on. The other class is fascinated by the fact that there is a living, feeling, emotional human being suffering from the sickness; and that his responses influence the progress of the malady, or even, in some cases, cause it. These are the more intelligent and thoughtful of doctors and Berg was one of them. Unfortunately in general practice it is difficult to devote enough time to unravelling the patient's emotional troubles and sooner or later such a physician feels frustrated. Berg himself says in his autobiography: 'I was getting tired of studying end-products, whether they were those of muscular movements, of skin rashes, or of visceral movement and change. How wonderful it would be if we could discover how those things started, what started them! And here were my patients or at least a majority of my patients, each offering me a clue to the investigation of this infinitely more important human problem.'

Thinking in this way it was inevitable that Berg should drift from general practice into psychiatry. He always insisted that he never appreciated that he was doing other than indulging his interest in the causation of illness, and not trying to carve out a career. Perhaps it was in the same way that Fritz Kreisler insisted that he played the violin because he enjoyed doing so and not because he wished to become a world famous virtuoso. However, it is not easy to change seats in mid-stream and the process was a gradual one.

Firstly Berg arranged with another doctor that he should share the practice so that he was free in the latter half of the day. This enabled him to study, attend lectures and study for the Diploma of Psychological Medicine. He attended a course at the Tavistock Clinic—where he was to work for some seventeen years—and at University College. There he met Professor J. C. Flugel who had a profound influence on him. He took a course for the D.P.M. at Bethlem Hospital merely because it was nearer. This was fortunate because the strongly organic bias at the Maudsley would have had the effect of making him rebel and perhaps turned him away from psychological medicine for ever.

No sooner had he passed the D.P.M. that Berg started to think of attacking the M.D. in psychological medicine. Curiously enough he was spurred on, not discouraged, by the remark of a doctor at Bethlem Hospital who said, 'But my dear chap, the M.D. in psychiatry is an examination for specialists, people who have worked in mental hospitals for years and years, and who have specialised in the subject.' The examination presented no difficulty to him and he passed it easily.

Now, although he was so well qualified, Berg felt disappointed. He says: 'Here was I, with an M.D. in psychological medicine and a D.P.M. still not knowing anything about the mind and its abnormalities, or even how to get down to providing any real help for the psychoneurotic patients.' This feeling is not unusual since the writer himself had the same experience.

Berg now started working seriously under Crichton Miller at the Tavistock Clinic. He started to learn how to treat psychoneurotic patients from the point of view of psychotherapy, whereas the M.D. and D.P.M. had merely taught him how to classify them, and the theories of the aetiology of their illness.

It was now time to undergo a personal analysis and Berg chose Professor Flugel for his analyst. He could not have chosen better for Flugel was immensely wise without forgetting he was a man of the world.

It was inevitable that as soon as he was able to change from general practice to psychotherapeutic work in Harley Street his time should become more and more occupied. Moreover, as time passed, he worked as physician to the British Hospital for Nervous Diseases and physician at the Institute for the Scientific Treatment of Delinquency.

However, although he worked so hard he still found opportunity to write articles which were mainly published in the *British Journal of Medical Psychology*. This finally led to the production of a book—*War in The Mind*—which he described as 'the Case-book of a Medical Psychologist'. It was one of those subtle books which look so simple at first glance—just a collection of stories about patients garnished with psychopathology but which terminated with the reader learning unconsciously a great deal about psychological illness, what causes it, and how it is cured. Naturally it was a great success.

Five years later, in 1946, he published *Deep Analysis* which was a clinical study of an individual case. This, similarly, was very successful and sold well. In 1948 he published *Clinical Psychology* and followed it up with *The Unconscious Significance of Hair*, and *The First Interview with a Psychiatrist*.

All these books were successful as publications and, I am sure, succeeded, also, in fulfilling his purpose of educating the public in a better understanding of psychogenic illness. Reading them one cannot avoid his spell: unlike the Ancient Mariner he never buttonholes one obviously, but comes with a story. Listening to it one absorbs his wise experiences without appreciating what one is doing.

In 1957 Berg published his autobiography—*Being lived by My Life* and in 1958 collaborated with Dr. A. M. Krich to produce *Homosexuality* in any English edition. He had promised to supply more material for an American book, but wrote to me saying that he had exhausted everything he had to say about the subject: would I supply the other half. Since he had recently had an operation (but no one knew then that he was suffering from a fatal cancer) I felt that perhaps it was poor Berg that was exhausted, and not the material; he had always had a bottomless supply of cases, and had never previously found it difficult to find what he needed. Naturally I promised at once to write my half of the book which was later published in America.

It was terrible, indeed, to hear from him in November 1957 to say that he was so seriously ill that he expected to live only two or three months. Characteristically his letter dealt mainly with a patient he had asked me to treat and with details of our joint book, rather than his own illness. It was the letter of a very brave man.

The eulogies of those who have died often have such a false ring that it is not easy to make the reader appreciate what a fine person Charles Berg was: fine as an individual, courteous, kind and friendly: he was the fine flower of English psychiatry, not absorbed in mechanical or chemical 'cures', which treat human beings as machines and suppress illness, but in understanding and treating his fellow men at the deepest level.

The influence of such a man spreads widely and lives long in the memories of his fellow workers and the lives of his patients.

GLOSSARY

AETIOLOGY
The science of causation.

AFFECT
The energy of an emotion. It may be aroused by a variety of stimuli and is capable of displacement on to concepts with which it was not originally associated.

ANTI-CATHEXIS
The shifting of an emotional charge (cathexis) associated with one impulse on to an impulse of an opposite character. For instance, an original emotional interest in soiling or dirtying may become an interest, often excessive, in cleanliness; and unconscious hate may appear as conscious love.

AUTO-EROTISM
Self-generated erotic stimulation without resort to another person.

DETUMESCENCE
Subsidence from swelling. A term much used by Havelock Ellis to denote what he calls the second part of physiological sexual activity. The first part, tumescence or becoming tumid, is followed, with or without orgasm, by a comparatively rapid subsidence of the tumidity with decline in excitation.

EFFORT SYNDROME OR INTOLERANCE
Palpitation, dizziness, shortness of breath and fatigue following moderate exertion.

EGO
That part of the id which has become modified by the impingement of external stimuli in such a way that it has become adapted to reality, reality testing and activity, and is credited with consciousness. In contradistinction to the id, it tends to organisation into a united whole.

EJACULATIO PRAECOX
A premature ejaculation of semen previous to, or at the beginning of coitus, and thus circumventing full orgastic satisfaction.

FETISH
Anything which is attractive on account of its association, usually through unconscious elements, with erotic pleasure.

HETEROSEXUALITY
Love for or erotic interest in a person of the opposite sex, i.e. normal psychosexual development.

HOMOSEXUALITY

Sexual desire for a member of the same sex.

ID

The concept of an undifferentiated primitive mind containing only innate urges, instincts, desires and wishes without consciousness or any appreciation of reality, and apparently dominated by the pleasure principle. Unlike the ego it is not organised or integrated, so that contrary and incompatible urges can exist side by side in it without necessarily entering into conflict with each other.

LIBIDO

The energy of the sexual instinct and of its psychosexual component instincts. It is subject to many vicissitudes. For example, it can become aim-inhibited (i.e. orgasm-inhibited) and undergo unlimited displacement even on to the person's own ego (narcissism, self-love), asexual objects and abstract ideas.

OBSESSIONAL NEUROSIS

A psychoneurosis characterized by the presence of obsessions which dominate the thought processes and behaviour of the patient. Compulsion neurosis.

OEDIPUS COMPLEX

As in the play (Oedipus Rex) by Sophocles, and as in the Greek legend on which it is founded, the unconscious of man from which these dramatizations originated, has been shown by psychoanalysis to contain a repressed constellation comprising a desire to displace the parent of the same sex and to possess sexually the parent of the opposite sex. It is something infinitely more powerful than common sense that comes into effective conflict with the Oedipus constellation. It is specifically fear of castration which causes total repression of these desires and phantasies. Amongst the evidences of this repression there are the normal horror of incest, intimacy with the very person with whom one had since birth or before birth been most intimate, and the normal tendency to dramatize the repressed constellation in actuality, through the mechanism of displacement, by marrying a person in the image of the repressed imago, and the persistence, at least in physical form, of a repugnance for those in the image of the once hated or displaced parent. Inability to deal adequately in these normal ways with the energy of the repressed complex and consequent regression to fixations at pre-Oedipus levels of libidinal organization, are the nuclear bases of psychoneurotic, characterological and mental disorders.

ORAL FIXATION

Arrest of a portion of the libidinal stream at the immature stage of development connected with the erotic feelings in babyhood, namely erotic excitation from stimulation of the mouth or lips.

PARASYMPATHETICOTONIA

Originally this term denoted a particular hyperirritability of the whole parasympathetic system, now it has become identical with vagotonia or excessive irritability of the vagus nerve which is said to be not uncommon in patients with schizophrenia. (Hinsie and Shatzky.)

PSYCHOPATHOLOGY

The study of morbidity in the psyche.

PSYCHOSIS

Insanity. Mental illness which includes the ego or reason and therefore the person's relationship to reality.

SUPEREGO

That part of the mental apparatus developed in early life by the mechanism of repressing frustrated impulses, such as aggression, and projecting them on the frustrators and subsequently introjecting them. Its function is largely to oppose the id, often unreasonably, and even to criticize and punish the ego if it tends to accept id demands. It is a sort of primitive unconscious conscience.

SYMPATHETICOTONIA

A condition in which there is increased tonus of the sympathetic system and a tendency to high blood pressure.

TUMESCENCE

A swelling-up. Specifically the turgidity produced in the sexual organs during the pre-orgasm stage of sexual excitement.

UNCONSCIOUS

A region of the psyche which contains mental processes and constellations which are ordinarily inaccessible to consciousness, commonly owing to the process of repression. The technique of mind analysis is especially designed to bring this unconscious material into consciousness by overcoming the resistances and repressing forces, as it is from the unconscious conflicts or complexes and their opposing forces or reaction formations that all symptoms emanate.

INDEX

For Product Safety Concerns and Information please contact our EU
representative GPSR@taylorandfrancis.com
Taylor & Francis Verlag GmbH, Kaufingerstraße 24, 80331 München, Germany